W9-ANY-836

Krac

AFRO-VEGAN

bryant terry

AFRO-VEGAN

FARM-FRESH AFRICAN, CARIBBEAN & SOUTHERN FLAVORS REMIXED

photography by Paige Green

TEN SPEED PRESS
Berkeley

Contents

Permission to Speak

BY JESSICA B. HARRIS

I smiled a lot as I read through the pages of *Afro-Vegan*, for in many ways it is a trip down memory lane. Reading it, I was taken back to the early days of my own work when I began to discover the culinary connections of the African Atlantic world as travel editor of *Essence* magazine in the 1970s. I recalled the first tastes of dishes sampled on the African continent that reminded me of those eaten in my grandmothers' kitchens and the ingredients that I saw in markets, which were also in my mother's larder.

As I paged through the manuscript, reading the text for what has become this beautiful book, it became a journey of recollections, much like the one that I indulge in monthly in my online radio show. Faces passed through my mind's eye. I recalled eating *tagine de légumes* in a *caïdal* tent in Marrakech, Morocco, and discovering that that country's *dada* was in many ways the equivalent of the South's mammys, a grand custodian of culinary traditions. I thought of my first Senegalese *thiebou dienn* and the connections it made to jollof rice, the Low Country's red rice and even southern Louisiana's jambalaya. I time-traveled to Brazil and the Caribbean and was transformed once again into the awkward young woman who spoke French and Spanish and Portuguese and liked to talk to old people in markets and taste what they had in their pots. My nostrils flared with the musty smell of old bookstores I'd visited and dusty archives where I'd researched. My mouth watered as I recalled the tastes of okra, black-eyed peas, and watermelon that were totems that marked the journey and all of the lessons learned. As I read Bryant Terry's proposed soundtracks, I heard the background music of my own journey: Maria Bethânia, Ornette Coleman, Zezé Motta, Celia Cruz, Gilberto Gil, Bembeya Jazz, Youssou N'Dour were amplified and complemented by other newer, younger voices. As I read the names of writers and artists mentioned, I mentally poured rum on the ground for the repose of those friends who are gathered at the table in the sky, and I raised a glass high in tribute to all those who are still creating the universe in which I am honored to live. In all of his work, Bryant Terry shows that he is certainly one of those by his commitment and dedication. In *Afro-Vegan*, he amply and ably demonstrates that he knows that food and culture are inseparable and that history is always there on the plate.

Bryant Terry named this "Permission to Speak," and I am delighted that he gave me the opportunity to so do. May his work continue to move us all closer, make us all healthier, and connect us all on the plate.

Introduction

Around the time I started writing this book, as a part of my research, I typed "African-American beans" into a search engine. I was expecting to view results about green beans, which often show up in traditional African-American cookery; red kidney beans, an emblematic legume of Louisiana Creole cuisine; and black-eyed peas, native to Africa and thought to bring prosperity throughout the year when eaten on New Year's Day. Instead, the first search result was for *Catfish in Black Bean Sauce*, a film about Vietnamese siblings raised by African-American parents. The second result was for "black (turtle) beans," and the next? Also "black beans." Not one of the ten results on that page was about the variety of beans and legumes historically grown and eaten by African-Americans. In many ways, that comically sad moment on the Internet symbolizes the invisibility and marginalization of food from the African diaspora that was a major impetus for writing this book.

A large part of my mission in writing *Afro-Vegan* is to move Afro-diasporic food from the margins closer to the center of our collective culinary consciousness and to put its ingredients, cooking techniques, and flavor profiles into wider circulation. But there is more to the story than that. Because these riches have been hardearned, underacknowledged, and even exploited, using them wisely means coming to terms with the problematic narratives that surround them. There is a notable failure to (1) acknowledge that the modern world is indebted to ancient Africans for basic farming techniques and agricultural production methods; (2) appreciate the agricultural expertise (rice production), cooking techniques (roasting, deep-frying, steaming in leaves), and ingredients (black-eyed peas, okra, sesame, watermelon) that Africans contributed to new world cuisine; and (3) recognize the centrality of African-diasporic people in helping define the tastes, ingredients, and classic dishes of the original modern global fusion cuisine—Southern food. You see, it is not enough to celebrate the food of the African diaspora without appreciating

the *people* who gave birth to this rich culinary heritage.

More than anyone else, people of African descent should honor, cultivate, and consume food from the African diaspora. Afro-diasporic foodways (that is, the shape and development of food traditions) carry our history, memories, and stories. They connect us to our ancestors and bring the past into the present day. They also have the potential to save our lives. As Afro-diasporic people have strayed from our traditional foods and adopted a Western diet, our health has suffered. Combined with the economic, physical, and geographic barriers that make it difficult to access *any* type of fresh food in many communities, the health of these populations across the globe has been devastated. In the United States, where I live and work, African-Americans suffer from some of the highest rates of preventable diet-related illnesses, such as heart disease, hypertension, and

type 2 diabetes. Many factors contribute to the increase in chronic illnesses affecting African-American communities, and I would argue that the disconnect from our historical foods is a significant contributing force. While we continue to work for food justice—the basic human right to fresh, safe, affordable, and culturally appropriate food in all communities—we must also work to reclaim our ancestral knowledge and embrace our culinary roots.

Culturally appropriate food is an important criterion for determining what is "healthy," and people of African descent need not look any further than our own historical foodways for better well-being. It is vital that we incorporate African and Afro-diasporic vegetables, grains, legumes, fruits, nuts, seeds, and cooking techniques into our kitchens. The nonprofit group Oldways: Health Through Heritage took a major step in illuminating the importance of eating African ancestral foods

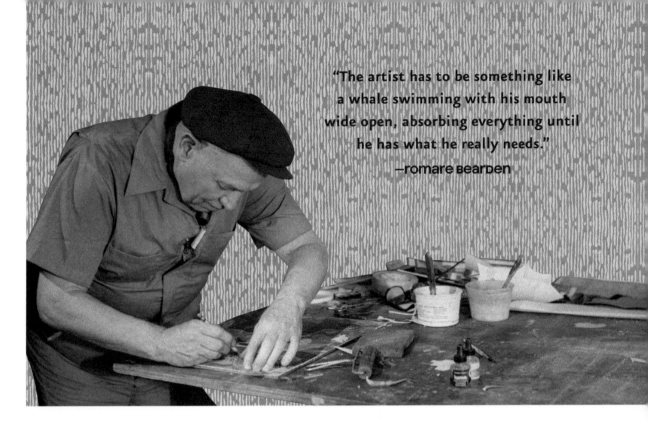

"The artist has to be something like a whale swimming with his mouth wide open, absorbing everything until he has what he really needs."

—ROMARE BEARDEN

when they created the African Heritage Diet Food Pyramid in 2011. This revision of the antiquated, one-size-fits-all food guide pyramid (which was finally abandoned by the United States Department of Agriculture in 2011 and replaced with the My Plate food guide) encourages us to consume lots of culturally appropriate leafy green vegetables, tubers, fruits, whole grains, legumes, seeds, and nuts. While this new guide is a great start, we still have much work to do.

Afro-Vegan is another tool for addressing the public health crisis among African-Americans that is directly related to what we eat. More and more, mainstream medical institutions have been acknowledging that the overconsumption of animal protein puts people at increased risk of preventable, diet-related illnesses, such as heart disease, type 2 diabetes, and hypertension, and an increasing number of medical professionals are endorsing plant-centered diets for optimal

health. This book continues in the tradition of my previous work by keeping one eye on contemporary health concerns while presenting food that honors the flavors, ingredients, and heritage of the African diaspora. *Afro-Vegan* will further empower people to choose wholesome foods to improve the physical and spiritual health of their families and communities.

African-American visual artist Romare Bearden once said, "The artist has to be something like a whale swimming with his mouth wide open, absorbing everything until he has what he really needs." In many ways, that quote has guided me through the process of writing this book over the past year. It should go without saying that what people of African descent have eaten for breakfast, lunch, and dinner since antiquity is complex and diverse. For this book, I devised a means of presenting the breadth and richness of Afro-diasporic food by creating culinary combinations inspired by home-cooked meals, cookbooks, restaurants, websites, narrative histories, scholarly monographs, and travel. While there is some emphasis on foods that are indigenous to Africa, ultimately, this book is about the fusion of food that resulted from food-crop exchanges between Africa and other parts of the globe that go back thousands of years.

Bearden's stunning collages are a major inspiration for *Afro-Vegan*. Just as he fused paint, magazine clippings, old paper, and fabric to visually reflect the African-American experience, I have blended vegetables, grains, legumes, fruits, nuts, and seeds to delve into the food history of the African diaspora. Imagine if you removed the animal products from African, Caribbean, Southern, and other Afro-influenced cuisines, then meticulously cut, pasted, and remixed the food to produce recipes with farm-fresh ingredients as their heart and soul: that is *Afro-Vegan*.

In these pages, you will find imaginative vegan recipes that highlight the interconnection, change, and growth of Afro-diasporic food over centuries. Quench your thirst with tart, sweet, and floral Roselle-Rooibos Drink (page 191), which combines tea made from Rooibos (the needlelike leaves of the South African Rooibos bush) with tangy-sour roselle leaves, which are used throughout West Africa and the Caribbean. Snack on Blackened Okra (page 30), which brings the *kingombo* (the Mbundu word for okra) of Central Africa across the ocean to Louisiana for a coating of piquant, smoky spices. Fill up with Savory Grits with Slow-Cooked Collard Greens (page 108), which combines the American South and East Africa in one warm bowl, topped with a dollop of Spicy Mustard Greens (page 25), a Southern-inspired version of harissa, the hot-pepper paste popular throughout North Africa. Satisfy your sweet tooth with Cocoa-Spice Cake with Crystallized Ginger and Coconut-Chocolate Ganache (page 174) while

enjoying flavors of the Caribbean—nutmeg, cayenne, coconut, avocado, rum, and ginger—with every bite. For each recipe, I've highlighted a few of the prominent ingredients to give you a sense of the dish's flavor profile.

Delicious as they are, these dishes do not stand alone—they are supported by culture, tradition, and memories. In fact, even the African Heritage Diet Food Pyramid emphasizes gardening, spending time with family, and building community around the table. When I reflect on my childhood (I grew up in Memphis, Tennessee, and spent summers in rural Mississippi) during the late 1970s and 1980s, I think fondly of gardening with my family, growing collards, mustards, turnips, butter beans, black-eyed peas, and green beans. I treasure my grandparents' home-cooked meals and preserves: pickled pears, peaches, green tomatoes, carrots, green beans, apples, figs, sauerkraut, blackberry jam, and chow-chow. And I maintain the core values that came from harvesting, sharing, preparing, and cooking meals with community. With all that in mind, I invited Michael W. Twitty, a renowned culinary historian of African-American foodways, to enrich my recipes with some gems about garden-to-table cooking. I also offer suggestions—with some help from my friends—for music, books, and films that complement the Afro-vegan eating experience.

I see this book naming and solidifying a new genre of cooking and eating, if you will—extending farm-fresh, compassionate food to include foods of the African diaspora. When you consider that for thousands of years traditional West and Central African diets were predominantly vegetarian—centered around staples like millet, rice, field peas, okra, hot peppers, and yams—and that many precolonial African diets heavily emphasized plant-based foods, a vegan cookbook celebrating the food of the African diaspora is perfectly fitting.

To be clear, *Afro-Vegan* is for everyone. I love feeding my diverse circle of family, friends, and fans vibrant and yummy home-cooked food that reflects my values around health, sustainability, compassion, and community building. This book's guiding philosophy is simple: lovingly prepared food with fresh, high-quality ingredients will always make a wholesome and delicious meal.

Although broad in geographic scope, this book is in no way comprehensive. Rather, these pages are a collection of more than one hundred fun and delicious recipes designed to nourish you—but also to inspire you. This is just a start. My hope is that you continue along this path to take the freshest, tastiest ingredients that you can find and create your own Afro-vegan dishes.

A FEW TIPS FOR ENJOYING THIS BOOK

Use good-quality sea salt, freshly ground white and black pepper, whole spices that you toast and grind as needed, fresh herbs, and seasonal produce (when possible) to get the most out of these recipes. This book honors the tradition of from-scratch cooking of our ancestors, and I invite you to make time to take your time. That said, I do understand if you need to use store-bought almond milk or vegetable stock in place of homemade.

Also, I firmly believe that recipes should be used as guides, and that spontaneity is one of the true pleasures of cooking. However, I ask that you make the recipes as written at least once before modifying them, so you get a sense of my desired flavors, textures, and spirit of the dish.

SPICES. SAUCES. HEAT.

IT GOES WITHOUT SAYING that fresh, seasonal fruits and vegetables provide the foundation for delicious, nourishing dishes. Oftentimes when I am cooking with food from a local farm, community plot, or my home garden, I like to keep it simple and let the natural flavors of the food shine through—olive oil, salt, fresh herbs, and pepper are all I need. However, when I really want to deepen and expand flavors, I use whole spices that I toast and pulverize in my mortar right before cooking.

The unique combination of herbs and spices in this chapter will take you on a culinary journey that will connect you with cuisines and cultures around the globe. Because cooking practices throughout Africa have traditionally been passed down orally, the ingredients, rituals around making food, and special ways of cooking can be as diverse as the local cultures across the continent. With this in mind, I offer my singular versions of spice blends, such as berbere, Jamaican curry powder, and za'atar, and I re-create popular sauces, such as North African chermoula and Memphis barbecue sauce. I also offer recipes for hot sauces that will refine the flavors of a dish and bring all of its elements together.

BERBERE

PAPRIKA, FENUGREEK, RED PEPPER FLAKES, CAYENNE, CHIPOTLE CHILE, BLACK PEPPER

YIELD about 1/3 cup

SOUNDTRACK "Hedetch Alu" by Mulugèn Mèllèssè from *Éthiopiques, Volume 10: Ethiopian Blues and Ballads*

6 cardamom pods

3 tablespoons paprika

1 tablespoon coarse sea salt

1 teaspoon cumin seeds, toasted (see sidebar, opposite)

1 teaspoon fenugreek seeds, toasted (see sidebar, opposite)

1 teaspoon allspice berries, toasted (see sidebar, opposite)

1 teaspoon red pepper flakes

1 teaspoon dried thyme

2 whole cloves

1 dried chipotle chile, stemmed, and broken into pieces

1 teaspoon black peppercorns

1/2 teaspoon coriander seeds, toasted (see sidebar, opposite)

1/2 teaspoon ground ginger

1/4 teaspoon ground nutmeg

1/4 teaspoon cayenne pepper

BERBERE, *a key spice blend in Ethiopian and Eritrean cooking, is used to season everything from vegetables to stews. As with most mixtures of spices, berbere has many variations and recipes depending on whom you ask, but its key ingredients include paprika, fenugreek, and dried chiles. The word "berbere" literally means "hot" in Amharic, the official language of Ethiopia, so there should be palpable heat in your mixture. But you can always tone down the amount of chile peppers to suit your needs. Although I initially created this particular blend for the purpose of seasoning Berbere-Spiced Black-Eyed Pea Sliders (page 32), I find myself using it to flavor stews, coat baked tofu, and punch up sautéed vegetable dishes. Sometimes I keep a tiny bowl of it near my sea salt and pepper grinder and use it as an all-purpose condiment. Two words: berbere popcorn. (Pictured on page 10.)*

Put the cardamom pods in a medium, dry skillet over medium-low heat. Toast until fragrant, shaking the pan occasionally to prevent burning, 2 to 3 minutes. Transfer the pods to a small plate, and set aside to cool. Once cooled, crack open the cardamom pods with your fingers and add their seeds to a mortar or spice grinder, then add the paprika, salt, cumin seeds, fenugreek seeds, allspice berries, red pepper flakes, thyme, cloves, chipotle, peppercorns, coriander seeds, ginger, nutmeg, and cayenne. Grind into a fine powder. Transfer to a jar and seal tightly. Stored at room temperature, it will keep for 6 months.

BLACKENED SEASONING

PAPRIKA, CUMIN, CORIANDER, BLACK PEPPER, WHITE PEPPER, GARLIC POWDER, ONION POWDER

YIELD about ⅓ cup | **SOUNDTRACK** "Let Your Yeah Be Yeah" by Buckwheat Zydeco from *Lay Your Burden Down*

2 tablespoons paprika

1 tablespoon cumin seeds, toasted (see sidebar)

2 teaspoons coriander seeds, toasted (see sidebar)

2 teaspoons black peppercorns

1½ teaspoons coarse sea salt

1½ teaspoons garlic powder

1 teaspoon white peppercorns

1 teaspoon onion powder

1 teaspoon dried thyme

½ teaspoon cayenne pepper, or to taste

BLACKENING *is a Cajun cooking technique (that spread throughout the South) in which food is coated with a medley of spices and cooked over very high heat, usually in a cast-iron skillet. This is a recipe for a spice mixture that I typically use for such purposes. The piquant, smoky blend adds a mouthwatering layer of flavor to blank-canvas foods like tofu, potatoes, and cauliflower, as in Blackened Cauliflower with Plum Tomato Sauce (page 76). If you like fiery heat, add more cayenne to your blend. (Pictured on page 11.)*

Combine the paprika, cumin seeds, coriander seeds, black peppercorns, salt, garlic powder, white peppercorns, onion powder, thyme, and cayenne in a mortar or spice grinder and grind into a fine powder. Transfer to a jar and seal tightly. Stored at room temperature, it will keep for 6 months.

TOASTING WHOLE SPICES

When working with farm- and garden-fresh produce, sometimes it's best to do as little as possible to the foods in order to let their natural flavors shine—lightly cooking and seasoning with a little salt and pepper often does the trick. But if you desire to add more complex flavors to your dishes, seek out commonly used spices like cayenne pepper, cinnamon, cumin, nutmeg, paprika, and red pepper flakes. If possible, use organic spices and look for them in the bulk section. They will be cheaper and this allows you to buy small amounts at a time, which ensures that you will use them up before they lose their intensity.

Although it might be convenient to use preground spices, toasting whole spices and grinding them right before using them will give you bolder and more complex flavors. The easiest way to toast spices is to heat a dry skillet over medium heat and add the spices after the pan is warm. Shake the pan to move the spices around and toast until they smell nutty and fragrant, usually 2 to 5 minutes. If toasting several spices for a recipe, do them in separate batches, since cooking times vary. Once the spices have cooled, pulverize them in a mortar or grind them in a spice grinder and use right away or store in an airtight container for up to 6 months.

Clockwise, from bottom left: BERBERE (PAGE 8), BASIL SALT (PAGE 13), JAMAICAN CURRY POWDER (PAGE 14), ZA'ATAR (PAGE 15), CREOLE SPICE BLEND (PAGE 12), BLACKENED SEASONING (PAGE 9)

CREOLE SPICE BLEND

GARLIC POWDER, PAPRIKA, ONION POWDER, CHILI POWDER, RED PEPPER FLAKES

YIELD about ⅓ cup	**SOUNDTRACK** "Creole" by Charlie Hunter Quartet (featuring Mos Def) from *Songs from the Analog Playground*

1 tablespoon garlic powder

1 tablespoon paprika

2 teaspoons coarse sea salt

2 teaspoons freshly ground black pepper

2 teaspoons onion powder

2 teaspoons chili powder

2 teaspoons red pepper flakes

1 teaspoon dried thyme

1 teaspoon dried oregano

½ teaspoon cayenne pepper

A COMBINATION OF *African, Caribbean, and Native American flavors, this spice blend serves as a metaphor for the melding of cultures during the seventeenth century when the French and Spanish occupied New Orleans. It pops up in classic dishes like étouffée, gumbo, and boiled shrimp and can also be used to season grains, vegetables, and stews. I use it to enhance the flavor of my Stewed Tomatoes and Black-Eyed Peas with Cornbread Croutons (page 53). (Pictured on page 11.)*

Combine all the ingredients in a mortar or spice grinder and grind into a fine powder. Transfer to a jar and seal tightly.

Stored at room temperature, it will keep for 6 months.

RECIPES FOR THE REVOLUTION

Afro-Vegan is an extension of the food activism that I began 2001. Since then, my guiding mantra has been, "start with the visceral, move to the cerebral, and end at the political." My cookbooks aim to challenge the way we compartmentalize the fight for a healthier food system. I see enjoying home-cooked meals with families and friends as a way to nourish our bodies, communally enjoy the sensual pleasures of the table, and activate our communities to regain control of our runaway food system.

BASIL SALT

SEA SALT, BASIL

YIELD about ¹/₂ cup

SOUNDTRACK "Salty Dog" by Jelly Roll Morton from *Jelly Roll Morton: The Complete Library of Congress Recordings*

¹/₄ cup coarse sea salt

¹/₄ cup packed minced fresh basil

I LOVE TO USE FRESH HERBS to enhance the flavor of salt. This version uses basil, but feel free to experiment with a different herb or a combination of herbs. By the way, these colorful blends make great gifts. (Pictured on page 10.)

Preheat the oven to 175°F. Line a small, rimmed baking sheet with parchment paper.

Combine the salt and basil in a spice grinder and process until finely ground. Spread the mixture on the lined baking sheet and bake for 15 minutes, stirring occasionally. Turn off the oven and leave the mixture in the oven to dry for 30 minutes.

Remove from the oven and let cool. Transfer to a jar and seal tightly. Stored at room temperature, it will keep for 6 months.

JAMAICAN CURRY POWDER

TURMERIC, CORIANDER, CUMIN, FENUGREEK, ALLSPICE, CAYENNE

YIELD about ½ cup

SOUNDTRACK "Jah Know" by Midnite from *Be Strong*

BOOK *Wake the Town and Tell the People: Dancehall Culture in Jamaica* by Norman C. Stolzoff

2 tablespoons ground turmeric

1 tablespoon coriander seeds, toasted (see sidebar, page 9)

1 tablespoon cumin seeds, toasted (see sidebar, page 9)

2 teaspoons fenugreek seeds, toasted (see sidebar, page 9)

2 teaspoons yellow mustard seeds, toasted (see sidebar, page 9)

2 teaspoons black peppercorns

1½ teaspoons allspice berries, toasted (see sidebar, page 9)

1 teaspoon ground ginger

¾ teaspoon cayenne pepper

2 whole cloves

CURRY POWDERS such as this are meant to evoke the complex and flavorful blending of herbs and spices in South Asian, Southeast Asian, and Caribbean cooking.

Like many edibles that have crossed the globe, the composition and preparation of curry powders vary depending on national and local traditions and family preferences. Jamaican curry developed as a result of the large Indian population in Jamaica that grew during the mid-nineteenth and early twentieth centuries, when Indians were brought to the island to work as indentured servants.

There are a few differences between Indian and Jamaican curry powders: Jamaican curry powders are bright yellow from lots of turmeric; they use allspice, a dried fruit that resembles peppercorns; and they most often include Scotch bonnet peppers, a variety of chile pepper found mainly in the Caribbean, instead of the chile peppers used in Indian curries. Since Scotch bonnet peppers are not easily found outside the Caribbean, I do not use them here. Feel free to add a touch if you have access to them. I use this blend in Curried Scalloped Potatoes with Coconut Milk (page 97), and it gives the dish an earthy character with a little bit of heat and faint sourness. You could also use it in soups, stews, marinades, and vegetable dishes. (Pictured on page 10.)

Combine all the ingredients in a mortar or spice grinder and grind into a fine powder. Transfer to a jar and seal tightly.

Stored at room temperature, it will keep for 6 months.

ZA'ATAR

THYME, OREGANO, SUMAC, CUMIN, SESAME, BLACK PEPPER

YIELD about ¹/₃ cup	**SOUNDTRACK** "Crescent" by the John Coltrane Quartet from *Crescent*	**BOOK** *ZaatarDiva* by Suheir Hammad

3 heaping tablespoons dried thyme

2 heaping tablespoons dried oregano

Scant 1 tablespoon ground sumac

1 teaspoon cumin seeds, toasted (see sidebar, page 9)

1 heaping tablespoon sesame seeds, toasted (see sidebar, page 119)

Freshly ground black pepper

ZA'ATAR is an old-world spice blend that is popular throughout the Middle East. Its usage dates back to ancient Egyptian and Levantine cultures. Typically, the blend includes toasted sesame seeds, thyme, sumac, oregano, marjoram, and salt. There are many variations and recipes, and blends can differ from region to region or even family to family. Thyme, one of the main ingredients, is often used medicinally. It's loaded with antioxidants and is a natural anti-inflammatory and antiseptic. (Pictured on page 11.)

Put the thyme, oregano, sumac, and cumin seeds in a mortar or spice grinder and grind into a fine powder. Add the sesame seeds and a few grinds of black pepper and stir well to combine. Transfer to a jar and seal tightly. Stored at room temperature, it will keep for 6 months.

A QUICK METHOD FOR DRYING FRESH HERBS

Preheat the oven to 175°F. Line a small, rimmed baking sheet with parchment paper. Spread up to 4 cups of herbs on the lined baking sheet. Bake for about 20 minutes, until dry and crumbly. Remove the stems and discard.

CHERMOULA

CUMIN, PAPRIKA, CAYENNE, BLACK PEPPER, SAFFRON, CILANTRO, PARSLEY

YIELD
about 3 cups

SOUNDTRACK "Les Ondes Orientales" by Dhafer Youssef Quartet from *Abu Nawas Rhapsody*

3 tablespoons extra-virgin olive oil

½ cup finely chopped red onion

1 teaspoon coarse sea salt

3 large cloves garlic, minced

1½ teaspoons cumin seeds, toasted (see sidebar, page 9) and ground

½ teaspoon paprika

¼ teaspoon freshly ground black pepper

⅛ teaspoon cayenne pepper

3 tablespoons freshly squeezed lemon juice

1 tablespoon freshly squeezed orange juice

2 tablespoons water

¼ teaspoon minced seeded habanero chile

Pinch of saffron threads, crumbled

1½ cups packed minced cilantro

½ cup packed minced flat-leaf parsley

CHERMOULA, AN HERB-FILLED SAUCE *used in Algerian, Moroccan, and Tunisian cooking, often serves as a marinade for fish and other meats. I thought it would make a tasty sauce in which to bake tempeh, and it does not disappoint. You could also try it on tofu or vegetables.*

Warm the oil in a medium sauté pan over medium-low heat. Add the onion and salt and sauté until the onion is soft, 5 to 7 minutes. Add the garlic, cumin, paprika, black pepper, and cayenne and sauté until fragrant, for 2 to 3 minutes. Set aside to cool slightly, about 5 minutes.

Add the lemon juice, orange juice, water, habanero, and saffron and mix until well combined. Stir in the cilantro and parsley. Taste and season with more salt if desired. Use immediately or store in a tightly sealed jar in the refrigerator for up to 1 week.

POMEGRANATE-PEACH BARBECUE SAUCE

TOMATO SAUCE, TOMATO PASTE, POMEGRANATE MOLASSES, CHIPOTLE CHILE, SAGE

YIELD about 2½ cups	**SOUNDTRACK** "Never Can Say Goodbye" by Isaac Hayes from *Black Moses*	**BOOK** *To Make Our World Anew: Volume I: A History of African Americans to 1880* edited by Robin D. G. Kelley and Early Lewis

3 tablespoons extra-virgin olive oil

½ cup finely chopped red onion

¼ teaspoon coarse sea salt

⅛ teaspoon cayenne pepper

1 large clove garlic, minced

1 cup diced peeled peaches

1 cup tomato sauce

¼ cup water

¼ cup red wine vinegar

¼ cup pomegranate molasses

3 tablespoons freshly squeezed lime juice

2 tablespoons tamari

2 tablespoons tomato paste

1 to 3 tablespoons chopped chipotle chile in adobo sauce

2 teaspoons minced fresh sage

BEING FROM MEMPHIS, *I've been a bit nervous about crafting a recipe for barbecue sauce. People take barbecue seriously in my hometown, and from all available evidence, Memphis-style barbecue sauce is better than any other. (I know, those are fightin' words.) In the past, I've created a barbecue-inspired marinade in which to bake tofu or tempeh, but this is my first attempt at making a proper sauce.*

Although this version is a bit thicker than a typical Memphis barbecue sauce, the important characteristics are all here: tomato based, tangy, and sweet from rich pomegranate molasses and fresh peaches. This sauce works well tossed with vegetables (see Roasted Parsnips in Barbecue Sauce, page 89), as a marinade for tofu (see Summer Vegetable and Tofu Kebabs, page 72), and cooked with beans (I feel a recipe for Baked Barbecue Black-Eyed-Peas from Vegan Soul Kitchen coming on).

Warm the oil in a small saucepan over medium heat. Add the onion, salt, and cayenne and sauté until the onion is soft, 5 to 7 minutes. Add the garlic and sauté until fragrant, 2 to 3 minutes.

Transfer to a blender. Add the peaches, tomato sauce, water, vinegar, pomegranate molasses, lime juice, tamari, tomato paste, and chipotle chile and process until smooth.

Pour the sauce back into the saucepan and simmer over medium-low heat, stirring occasionally, until thick, about 20 minutes. Stir in the sage and simmer for 1 to 2 minutes. Taste and season with more salt if desired. Use immediately or store in a tightly sealed jar in the refrigerator for up to 1 week.

CHIPOTLE-BANANA PEPPER SAUCE

RICE VINEGAR, CHIPOTLE CHILES IN ADOBO SAUCE, GARLIC

YIELD
about 1 cup

SOUNDTRACK "20 Feet Tall (Yoruba Soul Remix)" by Erykah Badu

¼ teaspoon extra-virgin olive oil

¼ cup finely diced red onion

1 large clove garlic, minced

½ teaspoon cumin seeds, toasted (see sidebar, page 9) and ground

¼ teaspoon coarse sea salt

1 to 3 teaspoons chopped chipotle chile in adobo sauce

½ cup rice vinegar

½ cup mashed banana

1 tablespoon water

½ teaspoon agave nectar

⅛ teaspoon freshly ground white pepper

I MADE THIS SAUCE *to be eaten with* Jamaican Patties Stuffed with Corn Maque Choux *(page 122). I use a rice vinegar so this sauce is not overly acidic; the chipotle gives it smokiness and just a hint of spiciness, and the banana adds a touch of sweet fruitiness.*

Warm the oil in a small saucepan over medium-low heat. Add the onion and sauté until soft, 5 to 7 minutes. Add the garlic, cumin, and salt and sauté until the garlic is fragrant, 2 to 3 minutes.

Transfer the mixture to a blender. Add the chile, vinegar, banana, water, and agave nectar and puree until smooth. Stir in the white pepper. Use immediately or store in a tightly sealed jar in the refrigerator for up to 1 month.

HOT-PEPPER VINEGAR

SERRANO CHILE, BLACK PEPPERCORNS

YIELD about 1 cup	**SOUNDTRACK** "Four Thieves Vinegar" by MF Doom from *Metal Fingers Presents Special Herbs*

4 serrano or other hot
chile peppers

4 black peppercorns

½ cup white vinegar

½ cup apple cider
vinegar

HOT-PEPPER VINEGAR *is a staple on many Southern tables. Sprinkling it over a mess of collard greens (or any other greens, for that matter) is the perfect way to season them, as the vinegar cuts some of the bitterness of the greens and brightens them up. The heat from the chiles makes any serving of greens more compelling!*

Sterilize a small bottle or canning jar with a capacity slightly over 1 cup. With a sharp knife, cut 2 slits into each chile. Put the chiles and peppercorns in the bottle. Put the vinegars in a small saucepan and bring to a simmer over medium heat. Immediately pour the vinegars into the bottle. Let cool slightly, then seal tightly and store in a cool, dark place for up to 1 month.

MANGO-HABANERO HOT SAUCE

MANGO, HABANERO CHILE, CHAMPAGNE VINEGAR, LIME JUICE

YIELD
about 1 cup

SOUNDTRACK "Hotter Than That" by Louis Armstrong from *The Complete Hot Five & Hot Seven Recordings, Volume 3*

2 teaspoons peanut oil

½ cup finely diced yellow onion

¼ cup thinly sliced carrot

1 teaspoon cumin seeds, toasted (see sidebar, page 9) and ground

¾ teaspoon coarse sea salt

⅛ teaspoon cayenne pepper

2 large cloves garlic, minced

¼ to 1 habanero chile, minced

½ teaspoon finely grated lime zest

½ cup diced ripe mango

¼ cup water

3 tablespoons champagne vinegar

2 tablespoons freshly squeezed lime juice

¼ teaspoon freshly ground white pepper

½ teaspoon minced flat-leaf parsley

THIS THICK CONDIMENT *provides a nice balance of sweet, savory, and spicy. The flavor is fantastic, and the combination of habanero, mango, and carrot gives the sauce a striking color. Although I made it specifically for Crunchy Bean and Okra Fritters (page 28), it would go well with all types of foods, from breakfast burritos to roasted russet potatoes. In the instructions I suggest adjusting the amount of habanero chile depending on the amount of heat you want. For even less heat, remove the seeds and veins before mincing the habanero (it's a good idea to wear gloves to do this). Even if the sauce is quite hot initially, I find that it tends to mellow after a few days.*

Warm the oil in a small saucepan over medium-low heat. Add the onion, carrot, cumin, salt, and cayenne and sauté until the onion just starts to brown, 8 to 10 minutes. Add the garlic, chile, and lime zest and sauté until the garlic is fragrant, 2 to 3 minutes. Add the mango, water, vinegar, lime juice, and white pepper and sauté until everything is warmed through, 2 to 3 minutes.

Transfer to a blender and puree until smooth. Taste and season with more salt if desired. Stir in the parsley. Use immediately or store in a tightly sealed jar in the refrigerator for up to 1 week.

SMOKY PILI PILI SAUCE

AFRICAN BIRD'S EYE CHILE, RED WINE VINEGAR, BOURBON, LEMON JUICE, ORANGE ZEST

YIELD	**SOUNDTRACK** "Angola" by Cesária Évora from	**BOOK** *Buck: A Memoir* by MK Asante
about 1 cup	*Miss Perfumado*	

1 tablespoon peanut oil

¼ cup finely diced white onion

2 teaspoons finely grated orange zest

2 large cloves garlic, minced

1½ teaspoons paprika

½ teaspoon coarse sea salt

2 to 6 African bird's eye chiles, seeded

¾ cup red wine vinegar

2 tablespoons freshly squeezed lemon juice

1 teaspoon bourbon

1 teaspoon maple syrup

½ teaspoon unsulfured molasses

1 teaspoon minced fresh basil

½ teaspoon freshly ground white pepper

AFRICAN BIRD'S EYE *chiles have grown wild in Malawi, South Africa, Ghana, Nigeria, Zimbabwe, and Mozambique for centuries, and they are the main ingredient in pili pili sauce, which is popular across Africa. I came up with the idea of adding bourbon to my version of this sauce after tasting Fire Dragon Love Sauce, made by my friends Gigi and Heather, in which they include mescal for smokiness. About the heat level: If I were using this sauce on something with a fairly mild flavor, such as Grilled Corn on the Cob (page 64) or roasted potatoes, I would make the sauce with just one or two chiles for a more toned-down version. But if I were pairing it with a heftier dish, for example, using it as a sauce for crunchy bean fritters, I'd probably include more chiles.*

Warm the oil in a small saucepan over medium-low heat, add the onion, and sauté until soft, 5 to 7 minutes. Add the orange zest, garlic, paprika, and salt and sauté until the garlic is fragrant, 2 to 3 minutes.

Transfer the mixture to a blender. Add the chiles, vinegar, lemon juice, bourbon, maple syrup, and molasses and puree until smooth. Pour the mixture back into the saucepan. Cover partially and simmer over low heat, stirring occasionally, until starting to reduce, about 30 minutes. Stir in the basil and white pepper and simmer for 2 minutes. Use immediately or store in a tightly sealed jar in the refrigerator for up to 1 week.

HARISSA

PAPRIKA, CAYENNE, RED PEPPER FLAKES, CUMIN, CORIANDER, TOMATO SAUCE, TOMATO PASTE

YIELD
about 1 cup

SOUNDTRACK "Harissa" by Afro Latin Vintage Orchestra from *Last Odyssey*

3 tablespoons extra-virgin olive oil

1 tablespoon paprika

1 tablespoon red pepper flakes

1 teaspoon cumin seeds, toasted (see sidebar, page 9) and ground

½ teaspoon coriander seeds, toasted (see sidebar, page 9) and ground

½ teaspoon coarse sea salt

¼ teaspoon cayenne pepper

1 serrano chile, seeded and minced

3 large cloves garlic, minced

¼ cup tomato sauce

2 tablespoons tomato paste

2 tablespoons water

1 tablespoon freshly squeezed lime juice

1 teaspoon maple syrup

¼ teaspoon freshly ground white pepper

HARISSA, A HOT-CHILE PASTE *commonly eaten in North Africa, is used in a range of dishes to add heat. I often make a saucier version with tomatoes to serves as a fiery dipping condiment, but here I present a thicker blend that can be used to flavor soups, stews, vegetables, and grain dishes.*

Warm the oil in a small saucepan over low heat. Add the paprika, red pepper flakes, cumin, coriander, salt, and cayenne and stir to combine. Cook, stirring occasionally, until fragrant, about 3 minutes. Stir in the serrano and garlic and sauté for 2 minutes. Add the tomato sauce, tomato paste, water, lime juice, and maple syrup.

Mix well and simmer, stirring occasionally, until the mixture starts to thicken, about 5 minutes. Stir in the white pepper. Taste and season with more salt if desired. Use immediately or store in a tightly sealed jar in the refrigerator for up to 1 week.

SPICY MUSTARD GREENS

CORIANDER, CUMIN, JALAPEÑO, PAPRIKA, CAYENNE, RED PEPPER FLAKES, CILANTRO, PARSLEY

YIELD
about 1 cup

SOUNDTRACK "Fantasy" by Ali Farka Touré and Toumani Diabaté from *Ali & Toumani*

1¼ teaspoon coarse sea salt

1 cup packed chopped mustard greens

3 tablespoons extra-virgin olive oil

3 cloves garlic, minced

½ teaspoon coriander seeds

½ teaspoon cumin seeds

6 tablespoons chopped jalapeño chiles

1 teaspoon smoked paprika

1 teaspoon red pepper flakes

¼ teaspoon cayenne pepper

1 tablespoon minced cilantro

1 tablespoon minced flat-leaf parsley

1 tablespoon freshly squeezed lemon juice

1 tablespoon red wine vinegar

2 teaspoons water

THIS IS A REALLY HOT *green version of harissa, the popular pepper paste used throughout North Africa. Jalapeños provide a spicy base and mustard greens give it peppery zest. I use it to season couscous and grains by incorporating a few tablespoons before adding water. It's also a wonderful spicy condiment for many dishes. If you need to tone the heat down, simply reduce the amount of jalapeño chiles and red pepper flakes (but then what's the point?—wink, wink).*

Put about 4 cups of water in a medium saucepan and bring to a boil over high heat. Add 1 teaspoon of the salt, then add the mustard greens. Return to a boil and cook uncovered until the greens are wilted, about 2 minutes. Drain well.

Warm the oil in a small skillet over low heat. Add the garlic and cook, stirring occasionally, until the garlic starts to turn golden, about 5 minutes. Transfer to a small heatproof bowl and set aside to cool.

In the same skillet, toast the coriander and cumin, shaking the pan occasionally, until fragrant. Let cool for a few minutes, then transfer to a mortar or spice grinder and grind into a fine powder.

Transfer the powder to a blender. Add the jalapeños, paprika, red pepper flakes, cayenne, cilantro, parsley, lemon juice, vinegar, water, mustard greens, garlic oil, and the remaining ¼ teaspoon salt. Puree until smooth. Taste and season with more salt if desired. Use immediately or store in a tightly sealed jar in the refrigerator for up to 1 week.

OKRA. BLACK-EYED PEAS.
WATERMELON.

OUTSIDE OF COLLARD GREENS, I imagine that the three ingredients most emblematic of African-American cooking are okra, black-eyed peas, and watermelon. I've always had a deep connection with them that started in my family's small farms and gardens, and I believe that they, more than any other foods, are a precious reminder of the interconnection of people of African descent across the globe. Evidence indicates that all three may have originated on the African continent and made their way to North America by way of the transatlantic slave trade. For me, these three ingredients not only symbolize the resilience and strength of the West and Central Africans who were taken from their homeland and transported across the ocean but also typify the seed-to-table food traditions that I celebrate in this book.

Okra is prized for its ability to thicken soups and stews and often shows up in the classic Louisiana dish gumbo and other Caribbean and Southern specialties. In this chapter I use it in fritters and also coat it with blackened seasoning, grill it, and serve it with red rice with a South Carolina twist. Black-eyed peas, a major source of protein in sub-Saharan Africa, are found throughout the continent and in North and South America. For this book, I transform them into tiny burgers seasoned with berbere, an Ethiopian spice blend, and also use them in a take on Texas caviar. Watermelon, which has been grown in Africa for centuries, has a complicated history in the American South. While it has long been a refreshing source of sustenance for African-Americans, it has also served as a symbol to racially stereotype black people. In my continual reclamation of this fruit, in this chapter I transform it into a cooling summer soup and an intriguingly spicy salad.

This chapter sets the tone for the remainder of the book. The reworking of ingredients and flavors is more than a material hybrid; these combinations also reveal the history of Africa's global presence.

CRUNCHY BEAN and OKRA FRITTERS with MANGO-HABANERO HOT SAUCE

BLACK-EYED PEAS, PEANUTS, RED ONION, CORNMEAL, THYME

YIELD 4 to 6 servings	**SOUNDTRACK** "For Dem Eye" (Ron Trent Juju Remix) by Seun Kuti and Egypt 80 from *From Africa with Fury: Rise Remixes*	**BOOK** *Americanah* by Chimamanda Ngozi Adichie

1 cup dried black-eyed peas, sorted and soaked in water overnight

1 cup skinless raw peanuts

½ red onion, finely chopped

1½ teaspoons fine sea salt

¼ teaspoon cayenne pepper

¼ cup plus 2 tablespoons water

1 tablespoon apple cider vinegar

1 tablespoon cornmeal

1 tablespoon minced fresh thyme

½ cup sliced okra, cut paper-thin

Coconut oil, for deep-frying (about 4 cups)

Mango-Habanero Hot Sauce (page 21), for serving

AS IN MY PREVIOUS TWO BOOKS, I've included a recipe for bean fritters. I just can't resist reinventing these tasty bites known as akara in Nigeria, acarajé in Brazil, and various other names throughout West and Central Africa and parts of the Caribbean, such as accra, akla, bean balls, bean fritters, binch akara, koose, koosé, kosai, kose, and kwasi. While I don't deep-fry often, I certainly don't avoid the cooking method altogether. In the context of a healthful diet, a deep-fried treat every now and then won't do much harm. In The Africa Cookbook, Jessica B. Harris explains, "Frying in deep oil, a traditional West African cooking technique, is one of the hallmarks of the food of the African-Atlantic world." I certainly appreciate the deep, rich flavor that it imparts.

Although bean fritters are often eaten as a breakfast item in Nigeria, they mostly show up as street food and snacks. I treat them as an appetizer here, to be enjoyed with sweet, creamy, and spicy Mango-Habanero Hot Sauce. However, you could certainly eat them as an entrée, with rice and vegetables alongside. The trick to making delicious, smooth fritters is removing the skins from all the black-eyed peas. Although this is time-consuming, it's worth the effort; try thinking of it as cooking meditation. It's a great party food, and I usually have one or two people help me with this task to speed things along. Traditionally, bean fritters are fried in palm oil, but I use coconut oil instead. If okra doesn't work for you, feel free to omit it.

Drain the black-eyed peas and rinse them well. Put them in a large bowl of water and vigorously rub them together, removing the skins as they float to the surface of the water. If the skins don't come off easily, peel or pop them off one by one. Drain well.

In a food processor fitted with the metal blade, combine the black-eyed peas, peanuts, onion, salt, cayenne, water, and vinegar. Pulse to make a completely smooth batter, scraping down the sides if necessary. Transfer to a bowl, cover, and refrigerate for at least 1 hour and up to 1 day.

Remove the batter from the refrigerator. Add the cornmeal and thyme and beat with a wooden spoon for 2 minutes. Stir in the okra.

Warm 3 to 4 inches of oil in a small saucepan over medium-high heat until hot but not smoking, about 375°F. Preheat the oven to 250°F. Line a plate with paper towels.

Scoop out a heaping tablespoon of batter and roll it into a walnut-size ball with your hands. Using a heatproof spoon, gently lower it into the oil. Fry fritters 4 at a time, stirring after 2 minutes, until golden brown, 4 to 5 minutes. If necessary, adjust the temperature to ensure that the fritters don't cook too quickly.

Using a slotted spoon, transfer the fritters to the lined plate to drain briefly, then transfer them to a baking sheet and keep warm in the oven until all have been cooked. Arrange the fritters on a platter and accompany with the hot sauce.

BLACKENED OKRA with RED RICE

BLACKENED SEASONING, TOMATO PASTE, TAMARI

YIELD 4 to 6 servings	SOUNDTRACK "Gumbo" by Zion I from *The Take Over*	BOOK *Searching for Zion: The Quest for Home in the African Diaspora* by Emily Raboteau

RICE

2 tablespoons peanut oil

½ cup finely diced yellow onion

½ teaspoon coarse sea salt

1 cup white basmati rice, soaked in water overnight and drained well

1 large clove garlic, minced

1 cup finely diced green bell pepper

5 tablespoons tomato paste

1¾ cups vegetable stock, homemade (page 42) or store-bought

2 teaspoons tamari

OKRA

1 teaspoon coarse sea salt

1 pound small to medium okra pods

2 tablespoons peanut oil

4 to 6 tablespoons blackened seasoning, homemade (page 9) or store-bought (see notes)

FOR YEARS, *I've been grilling okra as a way to make it palatable for those who have an aversion to its sliminess after being cooked. I find that roasting or grilling small pods tends to tone down the slime factor. Although okra is available almost year-round in many parts of the South, where it is most popular, in other parts of the country the best (and least-expensive) okra pops up during summer. I created this dish as a way to combine the spicy, intense flavor of Cajun blackened seasoning with mild-flavored okra. As a tasty snack or a side dish it will happily stand alone, but when combined with a simple red rice dish in a South Carolina style, this okra is stellar.*

To make the rice, warm the oil in a medium saucepan over low heat. Add the onion and salt and sauté until the onion is golden brown and quite soft, 10 to 15 minutes. Add the rice and cook, stirring often, until the water has evaporated and the rice starts to smell nutty about 2 minutes. Add the garlic and bell pepper and sauté until fragrant, about 2 minutes. Add the tomato paste and stir well to coat the rice and vegetables. Stir in the stock and tamari, increase the heat to high, and bring to a boil. Decrease the heat to low, cover, and cook until the liquid is absorbed and the rice is tender, about 15 minutes. Remove from the heat and let stand, covered, until the okra is ready.

To make the okra, prepare a medium-high grill (see notes). Put about 12 cups of water in a large pot and bring to a boil over high heat. Add the salt, then add the okra and blanch for 1 minute. Drain well.

Transfer to a large bowl, drizzle with the oil, and toss until evenly coated. Sprinkle with the blackened seasoning and toss again until evenly coated. Thread the okra pods onto skewers, putting about 6 pods on each skewer. Grill until browned and slightly crisp, 3 to 4 minutes per side.

To serve, cut each pod into thirds and serve atop the rice.

NOTES

- If serving the okra on its own, without the rice, use 6 tablespoons of the blackened seasoning; otherwise use 4 tablespoons of the seasoning.

- If grilling isn't feasible, you can broil the okra, placing the pods about 3 inches from the heat and cooking until browned, bubbling, and starting to crisp, 3 to 4 minutes per side.

BERBERE-SPICED BLACK-EYED PEA SLIDERS

PORTOBELLO MUSHROOM, BLACK-EYED PEAS, MILLET

YIELD 20 sliders; 10 servings	**SOUNDTRACK** "An Epic Story" by Mulatu Astatke and the Heliocentrics from *Inspiration Information 3*	**BOOK** *Yes, Chef: A Memoir* by Marcus Samuelsson

2 tablespoons extra-virgin olive oil, plus more for panfrying

1 cup diced red onion

3 cloves garlic, minced

5 teaspoons berbere, homemade (page 8) or store-bought

Fine sea salt and freshly ground black pepper

1½ cups finely chopped portobello mushrooms

1 cup panko bread crumbs

2 tablespoons tomato paste

3 cups cooked black-eyed peas, drained (see sidebar)

2 tablespoons tamari

2 tablespoons freshly squeezed lemon juice

1 tablespoon unsulfured molasses

1 tablespoon water

1½ cups cooked millet (see sidebar)

1 jalapeño chile, seeded and minced

2 tablespoons minced cilantro

Avocado and tomato slices, for serving

20 mini buns, toasted

Cumin-Pickled Onions (page 137), for serving

Dill-Pickled Mustard Greens (page 138) or Quick-Pickled Vegetable Salad (page 82), for serving

WHEN I WAS CONCEPTUALIZING this recipe, I decided that I would take the now-ubiquitous veggie burger and give it an Afro-diasporic twist. The first time I was testing it, I found that crafting tiny sliders worked better than large patties. Plus, it gave the burger a kid-friendly spin and made them party ready. The combination of black-eyed peas, portobello mushrooms, and cooked millet creates a hearty base, and the berbere spice mixture deepens the flavor. For a fun meal, pair them with Smashed Potatoes, Peas, and Corn with Chile-Garlic Oil (page 94) and, to take it over the top, Sweet Pickled Watermelon Rinds and Jalapeños (page 140).

Warm the oil in a small skillet over low heat. Add the onion and sauté until dark golden brown and extremely soft, about 30 minutes. Add the garlic, berbere, and ½ teaspoon salt and sauté until fragrant, about 2 minutes. Increase the heat to medium. Add the mushrooms, bread crumbs, and tomato paste and cook, stirring occasionally, until the mushrooms are soft, about 5 minutes.

In a food processor fitted with the metal blade, combine the black-eyed peas, tamari, lemon juice, molasses, and water. Process until smooth, scraping down the sides and pulsing if necessary. Transfer to a bowl and fold in the millet, jalapeño, cilantro, and mushroom mixture. Season with black pepper and, if desired, more salt. Refrigerate the mixture for 30 minutes.

Make 20 sliders, scooping out about ¼ cup of the mixture for each and forming it into a patty about 2½ inches wide and ¾ inch thick. Set them on a baking sheet and refrigerate for 30 minutes.

Pour enough oil into a large nonstick skillet to thinly coat the bottom. Warm over high heat until very hot. Add as many sliders as can fit in the pan without touching. Decrease the heat to medium and cook until browned and crispy, about 5 minutes each side. Set the cooked sliders on a baking sheet and continue until all are cooked.

To serve, mash a slice of avocado on the bottom half of each toasted bun, then top with a slider, a slice of tomato, a few slices of pickled onion, a generous mound of pickled greens, and the top half of the bun.

COOKING BLACK-EYED PEAS AND MILLET

This recipe calls for precooked black-eyed peas and millet, so here are recipes for both.

To yield 3 cups cooked black-eyed peas, soak 1 cup black-eyed peas in water overnight. Drain, then transfer to a medium saucepan and fill with enough water to cover the beans by 2 inches. Place over high heat and bring to a boil. Skim off any foam, reduce the heat to medium, partially cover, and simmer until the beans are softening but still firm, 40 to 50 minutes. Add 1 teaspoon salt and simmer for another 10 minutes. Drain the beans, rinse in cold water for 1 minute, and set aside to cool.

To yield 1^1/$_2$ cups cooked millet, soak a scant ^{1}/$_2$ cup millet in water overnight. Drain the millet, then transfer to a small saucepan and combine with a little more than 1 cup water. Bring to a boil over high heat, then quickly reduce the heat to low. Cover and simmer until the millet has absorbed most of the water, about 20 minutes. Turn off the heat and set aside, covered, to steam for about 10 minutes.

TEXAS CAVIAR on GRILLED RUSTIC BREAD

BLACK-EYED PEAS, TOMATO, BELL PEPPER, CRISPY GARLIC

YIELD 4 to 6 servings	SOUNDTRACK "Super Rich Kids" by Frank Ocean (featuring Earl Sweatshirt; Slim K. Chopped and Screwed Remix) from *Channel Purple*	BOOK *The Cutting Season: A Novel* by Attica Locke

2 whole sun-dried tomatoes, or scant ¼ cup diced sun-dried tomatoes

⅔ cup dried black-eyed peas, sorted and soaked in water overnight

1¾ teaspoons coarse sea salt

¾ cup extra-virgin olive oil

16 large cloves garlic, thinly sliced

2 tablespoons freshly squeezed lemon juice

2 tablespoons red wine vinegar

1½ cups diced seeded heirloom tomatoes, in ¼-inch pieces

1 cup diced green bell pepper, in ¼-inch pieces

½ cup diced yellow bell pepper, in ¼-inch pieces

¼ cup diced red onion, in ¼-inch pieces

2 jalapeño chiles, seeded and diced into ¼-inch pieces

½ cup packed minced cilantro

Freshly ground black pepper

1 large loaf rustic bread, cut into about twelve ½- to ¾-inch-thick slices

ONE OF THE MANY *creative ways that Southerners use black-eyed peas is to combine them with tomato, bell pepper, and onion and tossing with a tangy vinaigrette to create Texas caviar. Although often eaten as a dip with chips, as one would enjoy tomato salsa, I spoon mine on thick slices of rustic bread that have been grilled or toasted and garnish each slice with crispy garlic and garlic oil, which makes for a party-perfect appetizer. This recipe yields a large quantity with summer gatherings in mind. Red Summer cocktails (page 195) would be the perfect accompaniment.*

Put the sun-dried tomatoes in a small heatproof bowl and add boiling water to cover. Cover and let soak for 5 minutes.

Drain the black-eyed peas and rinse them well. Transfer to a medium saucepan and add water to cover by 2 inches. Bring to a boil over high heat. Decrease the heat to medium, skim off any foam, and partially cover. Cook until the beans are softening but still firm, 40 to 50 minutes. Stir in 1 teaspoon of the salt and simmer for 10 minutes. Drain in a colander, rinse under cold water for 1 minute, and let cool.

Meanwhile, warm the oil in a medium skillet over low heat. Add the garlic and cook, stirring occasionally, until crispy and golden brown, 8 to 10 minutes. Strain the garlic oil through a fine-mesh sieve into a bowl and reserve the garlic and the oil separately.

Drain the sun-dried tomatoes, chop finely, and put in a blender. Add the lemon juice, vinegar, and the remaining ¾ teaspoon salt and process until smooth. With the blender running, pour in ¼ cup of the garlic oil in a slow stream and process until creamy.

Transfer the blended mixture to a large bowl. Add the black-eyed peas, tomatoes, green and yellow bell peppers, onion, jalapeños, and half of the cilantro. Stir gently until well combined, then cover and let rest at room temperature for 1 hour.

Preheat the oven to 400°F. Season the black-eyed pea mixture with black pepper and, if desired, more salt.

Lightly brush each slice of bread with garlic oil, saving any leftover for drizzling. Put the bread on a large baking sheet and bake, without turning, until lightly browned and toasted on top, 6 to 10 minutes. Top each slice with 2 heaping tablespoons of the black-eyed pea mixture. Garnish with a few slices of crispy garlic and a scattering of the remaining cilantro. Drizzle with garlic oil and enjoy.

CHILLED WATERMELON SOUP and
QUICK-PICKLED CUCUMBER with MINT

CUCUMBER, RED WINE VINEGAR, EXTRA-VIRGIN OLIVE OIL

YIELD 4 to 6 servings || **SOUNDTRACK** "Snowman" by Martina Topley Bird from *Some Place Simple*

PICKLED CUCUMBER

- 1 large English cucumber, peeled and diced into ¼-inch pieces
- 1 teaspoon coarse sea salt
- 1 cup rice vinegar
- 1 cup water
- ¼ cup raw cane sugar
- 1 teaspoon black peppercorns
- 2 tablespoons chopped fresh mint

SOUP

- 8 cups seeded diced yellow watermelon flesh (about 1 pound), refrigerated overnight
- 2 tablespoons red wine vinegar
- 1 tablespoon extra-virgin olive oil
- ¾ teaspoon coarse sea salt
- 2 to 3 cups large ice cubes

THIS IS A SOUP *best served as a midafternoon snack when the sun is at its peak on one of those so-sweltering-hot-you-barely-want-to-move-let-alone-cook days. Refreshing and cooling, this pureed watermelon topped with a quick-pickled play on the Algerian salade de concombre à la menthe* can be prepared the night before for minimal work the day of a heat wave. I call for yellow watermelon for a change of pace, but you can always use red. When prepping the watermelon, consider setting aside the rind for use in Sweet Pickled Watermelon Rinds and Jalapeños (page 140).

To prepare the cucumber, put the cucumber in a medium bowl and sprinkle with the salt. Toss until the salt is evenly distributed. Set aside for 5 minutes. Transfer to a colander. (Rinse the bowl clean and set it aside.) Put the colander in the sink and let drain for 30 minutes. Rinse the cucumber under cold water and return them to the bowl.

Meanwhile, combine the rice vinegar, water, sugar, and peppercorns in a medium sauté pan over low heat. Cook, stirring frequently, until the sugar is completely dissolved, about 3 minutes. Remove from the heat and let cool completely. Pour over the cucumber and let

sit for at least 1 hour. Just before serving, drain the cucumber, add the mint, and toss gently to combine.

To make the soup, put the watermelon in a blender and puree until smooth. Strain through a medium-mesh strainer into a pitcher to remove the seeds. Stir in the red wine vinegar, oil, and salt.

To serve, put ½ cup of the ice cubes in each bowl. Pour in the soup and top with 2 heaping tablespoons of pickled cucumber. Serve in chilled bowls, and don't hesitate to eat the ice cubes!

STRABERRY-WATERMELON SALAD with BASIL-CAYENNE SYRUP

BASIL, LIME JUICE, SEA SALT

YIELD 4 to 6 servings | **SOUNDTRACK** "I'm Happy" by Osunlade from *Pyrography* | **BOOK** *Songs in the Key of My Life: A Memoir* by Ferentz Lafargue

4 cups strawberries

6 ounces watermelon flesh

¼ cup packed minced fresh basil

2 tablespoons Basil-Cayenne Syrup (page 185)

2 tablespoons freshly squeezed lime juice

⅛ teaspoon Basil Salt (page 13), or to taste

THIS IS A DELICIOUS *and refreshing fruit salad. The Basil-Cayenne Syrup makes it garden party worthy, but you could easily eat it without the sweet-spicy dressing as an everyday treat. When prepping the watermelon, consider setting aside the rind for use in Sweet Pickled Watermelon Rinds and Jalapeños (page 140).*

Quarter the strawberries lengthwise and put them in a large bowl. Seed the watermelon and cut it into small, triangular wedges about the size of the strawberry slices and add to the bowl with the strawberries. Add the basil and 2 tablespoons of the syrup and stir gently to combine. Taste and add more syrup if desired. Cover and refrigerate until chilled, at least 1 hour.

Just before serving, remove the salad from the refrigerator and drizzle with the lime juice. Toss gently to combine. Sprinkle with the Basil Salt and serve immediately.

SOUPS. STEWS. TAGINES.

IN SOME WAYS I see this as the most important chapter of this book. For one, hearty soups and stews are vitally important to a healthful, plant-centered diet. Packing them with nutrient-dense vegetables (which have some protein), plus beans, tempeh, tofu, and nut pastes will ensure that our bodies are receiving a variety of amino acids for optimal health. The other reason this chapter is so crucial to the narrative of this book is the role that soups and stews have historically played in sub-Saharan Africa.

In *The Africa Cookbook*, Jessica B. Harris recounts how the main dish in meals on much of the African continent is a thick or soupy stew with a starch. Although some of the soups in this chapter were created for the purpose of starting a more substantial dinner or for serving as a light meal, in the spirit of the soup-, sauce- and stew-centered meals commonly eaten in sub-Saharan Africa, the stews and tagines in *Afro-Vegan* serve as nourishing centerpieces to be eaten along with starches and sides for a hearty meal.

I also see this chapter providing the foundation for cooking your own ingredient-driven soups, stews, and tagines. Search out fresh, seasonal ingredients from your home garden or community garden, a local farm or farmers' market, and locally owned grocery stores to create new recipes, using the cooking techniques in these recipes to assist you. Soups and stews are so easily adaptable, and I envision you modifying these recipes depending on season, geographic region, and personal preferences. For example, the Tofu Curry with Mustard Greens (page 54) could easily be modified to use tempeh and collard greens. In the Creamy Coconut-Cashew Soup (page 48), summer's bounty of okra, corn, and tomatoes could be replaced with a mixture of winter root vegetables, such as parsnips, turnips, and sweet potatoes. In the Sweet Potato and Pumpkin Soup (page 47), butternut squash might be substituted for the sweet potatoes and pumpkins.

SIMPLE VEGETABLE STOCK

CABBAGE, CARROT, CELERY, ONION, GARLIC

YIELD about 7 cups

SOUNDTRACK "Smilin' Billy Suite Pt. II" by The Heath Brothers from *Marchin' On*

½ small head of green cabbage (about 1 pound), thinly sliced

1 large carrot, coarsely grated

2 stalks celery, thinly sliced

2 large yellow onions, thinly sliced

1 head garlic, broken apart into cloves and unpeeled cloves smashed with the flat side of a knife

3 sprigs thyme

½ teaspoon coarse sea salt

9 cups water

A NUMBER OF RECIPES *in this book call for homemade stock, but I would not be mad if you used the best-quality boxed stock you can find. I simply think you will get the most flavor from these recipes if you use fresh stock. It's simple yet flavorful, and you can make a big batch and freeze it until you need it. In the past, I would cut the vegetables into chunks, but I find that thinly slicing and grating the vegetables makes for a much more flavorful stock.*

Combine all the ingredients in a large pot and bring to a boil over medium-high heat. Decrease the heat to medium-low and simmer uncovered for about 1 hour. Strain through a fine-mesh sieve, pressing down on the solids to extract as much liquid as possible. (Compost the solids.) Use immediately or let cool and store in the refrigerator for up to 3 days or the freezer for up to 6 months.

CORN BROTH

SWEET CORN, SALT

YIELD about 7 cups

SOUNDTRACK "Capricorn" by Miles Davis from *Water Babies*

BOOK *A Small Place* by Jamaica Kincaid

4 to 6 cobs from fresh sweet corn, broken in half

9 cups water

Coarse sea salt

GREAT FOR SIPPING on hot days and adding depth to soups and stews, this broth is also a good way to get the most out of corncobs. After making Grilled Corn on the Cob (page 64), Smashed Potatoes, Peas, and Corn with Chile-Garlic Oil (page 94), and Jamaican Patties Stuffed with Corn Maque Choux (page 122), you can store leftover cobs in the freezer until you're ready to make this broth.

Put the corncobs and water in a large pot and bring to a boil over high heat. Decrease the heat to medium-low, partially cover, and simmer for 45 minutes. Strain through a colander. (Compost the cobs.) Season with salt to taste. Use immediately or let cool and store in the refrigerator for up to 3 days or the freezer for up to 6 months.

HOMINY and SPINACH in TOMATO-GARLIC BROTH

TOMATO, PARSLEY

YIELD 4 to 6 servings

SOUNDTRACK "Original Syncro System" by Sunny Ade and His African Beats from *Syncro System Movement*

BOOK *The Famished Road* by Ben Okri

1 cup dried small hominy, soaked in water overnight and drained well

2 tablespoons extra-virgin olive oil

½ cup diced carrot

½ cup diced red onion

¼ teaspoon coarse sea salt

7 cloves garlic, minced

1 (28-ounce) can plum tomatoes with juices, chopped

5 cups vegetable stock, homemade (page 42) or store-bought

Sunflower oil, for deep-frying (about 4 cups)

1 cup packed minced spinach

Freshly ground white pepper

2 tablespoons minced flat-leaf parsley

THIS SOUP IS PRIMARILY *inspired by the ingredients and flavor profile of a version of efo riro, a traditional Yoruban stew eaten in Nigeria that I ate several years ago. It was loaded with fresh spinach and tomatoes and included a bit of pounded yam for starchiness. The base of this soup is a smooth tomato-garlic broth that's combined with minced spinach and hominy, the latter a traditional Native American staple that shows up in both African-American and Afro-Caribbean cuisine.*

Put the hominy in a medium saucepan and add enough water to cover by 2 inches. Bring to a boil over high heat. Decrease the heat to low, cover, and simmer until tender, 1½ to 2 hours. Drain well. Transfer ³/₄ cup of the cooked hominy to a clean kitchen towel and rub gently to dry more thoroughly.

To make the broth, warm the oil in a large saucepan over medium-low heat. Add the carrot, onion, and salt and sauté until the vegetables are soft but not browning, 5 to 7 minutes. Add the garlic and sauté until fragrant, 2 to 3 minutes. Stir in the tomatoes and stock. Increase the heat to medium-high and bring to a boil. Immediately decrease the heat to medium-low, partially cover, and simmer until starting to thicken, about 45 minutes.

Meanwhile, line a plate with paper towels. Warm about 2 inches of sunflower oil in a small saucepan until hot but not smoking (about 375°F), about 5 minutes. Gently add half of the dried ³/₄ cup hominy. Fry, stirring occasionally, until lightly golden, 4 to 5 minutes. Using a slotted spoon, transfer to the lined plate to drain. Repeat with the remaining dried hominy.

Strain the broth through a fine-mesh sieve, pressing down on the solids to extract as much liquid as possible. (Compost the solids.) Return the broth to the saucepan and stir in the unfried hominy. Place over medium-low heat, bring to a simmer, and cook for 10 minutes. Stir in the spinach, cover, and cook for 1 minute. Season with salt and pepper to taste. Serve topped with 2 heaping tablespoons of fried hominy and garnished with the parsley.

SWEET CORN and GINGER SOUP

COCONUT MILK, CARROT, CELERY, CILANTRO

YIELD 4 to 6 servings | **SOUNDTRACK** "Ba Da" by Gregory Isaacs from *The Ruler 1972-1990: Reggae Anthology*

1 tablespoon coconut oil

1 cup finely diced yellow onion

½ cup diced carrot

¼ cup finely diced celery (strings removed before dicing; see sidebar, page 74)

1 tablespoon minced fresh ginger

1 clove garlic, minced

½ teaspoon paprika

½ teaspoon coarse sea salt

4½ cups Corn Broth (page 43)

1 cup coconut milk

Kernels from 6 ears of sweet corn

Freshly ground white pepper

3 tablespoons chopped cilantro

THE COMBINATION *of fresh corn, ginger, and coconut milk gives this soothing and hydrating soup a Caribbean twist. A big bowl of it with a piece of cornbread or crusty bread makes a perfect light lunch on a hot day. Consider cutting the kernels off the corncobs a bit in advance so you can use the cobs to make the Corn Broth.*

Warm the oil in a medium saucepan over medium heat. Add the onion, carrot, celery, and ginger and sauté until the vegetables are soft, 5 to 7 minutes. Add the garlic, paprika, and ½ teaspoon of salt and sauté, until fragrant, 2 to 3 minutes. Stir in the broth and coconut milk. Decrease the heat to low, cover, and simmer for 20 minutes.

Working in batches if need be, transfer to a blender and process until creamy. Strain through a fine-mesh sieve back into the saucepan, pressing down on the solids to extract as much liquid as possible. (Compost the solids.) Add the corn and cook, over medium-low heat stirring occasionally, for 5 minutes. Season with salt and pepper to taste. Garnish with the cilantro before serving.

SWEET POTATO and PUMPKIN SOUP

PUMPKIN SEEDS, CINNAMON, CASHEWS

YIELD 4 to 6 servings | **SOUNDTRACK** "Africaine" by Art Blakey & The Jazz Messengers from *Africaine*

Ingredients:

- 1 small pumpkin (about 2 pounds)
- 1 teaspoon extra-virgin olive oil
- 5 cups vegetable stock, homemade (page 42) or store-bought
- 1 (2-inch) cinnamon stick
- ½ teaspoon coarse sea salt
- 2 sweet potatoes (about 1½ pounds total), peeled and cut into 1-inch pieces
- 1 cup Creamed Cashews (page 143)
- Freshly ground white pepper

THIS SILKY WINTER SOUP *combines pumpkin—used in soups and stews throughout Africa—and sweet potatoes, which are emblematic of African-American foodways. It's great hot or at room temperature, and the addition of toasted pumpkin seeds lends a nice textural accent.*

Preheat the oven to 275°F. Line a small, rimmed baking sheet with parchment paper.

Cut the top off the pumpkin and scoop out the seeds. (It is fine if the seeds have some remnants of squash on them.) Put the seeds in a small bowl, drizzle with the oil, and toss until evenly coated. Spread the seeds in a single layer on the lined baking sheet and bake for about 15 minutes, until lightly browned, stirring every 5 minutes for even cooking. Set aside.

Meanwhile, peel the pumpkin and cut it into 1-inch pieces. Put the stock, cinnamon stick, and salt in a large saucepan over medium heat and bring to a simmer. Cook for 5 minutes, then add the pumpkin and sweet potatoes. Increase the heat to high and bring to a boil. Immediately decrease the heat to medium-low, cover, and simmer, stirring occasionally, until the vegetables are fork-tender, about 35 minutes. Stir in the cashew cream.

Using a standard blender and working in batches, or using an immersion blender, blend the soup until smooth. Pour the soup back into the saucepan and cook, over medium-low heat, stirring occasionally, until warmed through. If necessary, thin with water so the soup pours easily from a spoon. Season with salt and pepper to taste. Serve garnished with the toasted pumpkin seeds.

NOTE: Toasted pumpkin seeds (and seeds of other winter squashes) can be eaten as a snack. If making them for that purpose, consider sprinkling with dried spices and herbs before toasting.

CREAMY COCONUT-CASHEW SOUP
with OKRA, CORN, and TOMATOES

COCONUT MILK, CASHEWS, PEANUTS, SUN-DRIED TOMATOES

YIELD 4 to 6 servings

SOUNDTRACK "Novo Dia" by Balança Povo from *Black Rio, Volume 2 Brazil Soul Power 1968-1981*

¼ cup packed diced sun-dried tomatoes

½ cup raw cashews

¼ cup skinless raw peanuts

2 tablespoons peanut oil

1 cup finely diced yellow onion

2½ teaspoons coarse sea salt

1 clove garlic, minced

6 cups Corn Broth (page 43) or vegetable stock, homemade (page 42) or store-bought

24 small to medium okra pods

Kernels from 4 large ears of sweet corn (store the cobs in the freezer to make Corn Broth, page 43)

¼ cup coconut milk

Freshly ground white pepper

¼ cup packed chopped flat-leaf parsley

INSPIRED BY VATAPÁ, *a Brazilian dish popular in Bahia, this soup is rich and creamy thanks to the cashews, peanuts, peanut oil, and coconut milk. I add the classic Southern combination of okra, corn, and tomatoes to make this a wonderful summer dish. Enjoy with crusty bread or a grain.*

Put the sun-dried tomatoes in a small heat proof bowl and add enough hot water to cover. Let sit for 5 minutes. Drain the sun-dried tomatoes. In a food processor fitted with the metal blade, combine the cashews, peanuts, and sun-dried tomatoes. Process into a chunky paste, scraping down the sides if necessary.

Warm 1 tablespoon of the oil in a medium saucepan over medium-low heat. Add the onion and ¾ teaspoon of the salt and sauté until the onion is soft, 5 to 8 minutes. Add the garlic and sauté until fragrant, 2 to 3 minutes. Stir in the cashew mixture and stock. Cover partially, bring to a gentle simmer, and cook, stirring occasionally, for 30 minutes.

Meanwhile, prepare the okra. Position an oven rack at the top level and preheat the broiler. Put about 8 cups of water in a medium pot and bring to a boil over high heat. Add 1 teaspoon of the salt, then add the okra and blanch for 1 minute. Drain well and pat dry with a clean kitchen towel.

Put the okra in a large bowl. Drizzle with the remaining 1 tablespoon oil and toss until evenly coated. Sprinkle with the remaining ½ teaspoon salt and toss again until evenly coated. Transfer to a rimmed baking sheet and broil until browning, bubbling, and starting to crisp, 3 to 4 minutes per side.

Add the corn and coconut milk to the saucepan. Puree the soup in batches in a blender or an immersion blender. Return the soup to the saucepan and warm over medium heat for a few minutes, until hot. Season with white pepper and, if desired, more salt. Garnish each serving with 4 or 6 pods of the okra and a sprinkling of the parsley.

BLACK BEAN and SEITAN STEW

VEGETABLE STOCK, ONION, GARLIC, GREEN BELL PEPPER, SCALLIONS

YIELD 6 to 8 servings

SOUNDTRACK "Ponta de Areia" by Wayne Shorter (featuring Milton Nascimento) from *Native Dancer*

1½ cups black beans, sorted and soaked in water overnight

6½ cups vegetable stock, homemade (page 42) or store-bought

1 bay leaf

½ cup plus 2 tablespoons extra-virgin olive oil

½ cup yellow cornmeal

½ teaspoon freshly ground black pepper

¼ cup apple cider vinegar

8 ounces seitan, cut into ½-inch-thick medallions

½ cup finely chopped white onion

4 large cloves garlic, minced

1 cup finely diced green bell pepper

1 scallion, white and green parts, finely chopped

1 cup tomato sauce

1 tablespoon tomato paste

½ teaspoon whole allspice berries, toasted (see sidebar, page 9) and ground

1½ teaspoons fine sea salt

2 tablespoons minced cilantro

Salty Lemon Cream with Parsley (page 146), for serving

BRAZIL HAS THE MOST people of African descent outside of the African continent itself, and African culture continues to thrive in the country's music, religion, and food. This stew is inspired by feijoada, which is considered the national dish of Brazil. My version pays homage to the close to 4 million enslaved Africans brought to Brazil by the Portuguese between the sixteenth and nineteenth centuries. While some argue that feijoada is a modified version of a slow-cooked casserole from Portugal containing beans and meat, legend has it that feijoada was created by enslaved Africans, who used the rice and bean rations that they were given as a base and augmented them with discarded parts of pigs (ears, feet, snouts, and innards) to add more heft. This meatless version gives a healthy nod to that rich history.

I don't cook with seitan often, but I use it here to provide the heartiness feijoada typically gets from beef and pork. If you are sensitive to or intolerant of wheat or gluten, you can substitute panfried tempeh for the seitan. Serve with white or brown rice, Muscovado-Roasted Plantains (page 62), Collards and Cabbage with Lots of Garlic (page 78), and Citrus Salad with Arugula (page 71).

Get the beans started by draining them, rinsing them well, and draining them again. Put the beans, stock, and bay leaf in a large pot. Bring to a boil over high heat. Decrease the heat to medium-low, partially cover, and simmer, stirring occasionally.

Meanwhile, warm the 2 tablespoons oil over medium-low heat. Add the onion and sauté until golden brown and quite soft, 10 to 15 minutes. Add the garlic and sauté until fragrant, about 3 minutes.

Stir in the bell pepper, scallions, tomato sauce, tomato paste, allspice, and 1 teaspoon salt and cook, stirring occasionally, until the bell pepper is soft, 3 to 5 minutes.

Stir the vegetable mixture into the beans and continue cooking the beans.

After the beans have been cooking for 1 hour, season with salt and black pepper to taste, and cook the stew, stirring occasionally, about 20 minutes more, until the beans are just tender. If necessary, add a little stock or water if the stew is too thick.

Combine the cornmeal, $1/2$ teaspoon of the salt, and the pepper in a small bowl and stir with a fork. Put the vinegar in a separate small bowl. One at a time, dip the seitan medallions into the vinegar, then roll them in the cornmeal mixture until evenly coated. Set the coated pieces on a plate.

Line a plate with paper towels. Warm the remaining $1/2$ cup oil in a large sauté pan over medium-high heat until hot but not smoking. Add the seitan and fry until golden brown and crispy, 1 to $1^1/2$ minutes on each side. Transfer to the lined plate to drain.

Serve with 4 to 5 pieces of seitan on top, garnished with the cilantro with the lemon cream alongside.

PEANUT STEW with WINTER VEGETABLES and CORNMEAL DUMPLINGS

CARROT, POTATO, PARSNIP, SWEET POTATO, TOMATO PASTE, PEANUT BUTTER

YIELD 4 to 6 servings	**SOUNDTRACK** "Ghana Emotion" by Omar from *Sing (If You Want It)*

STEW

- 1 tablespoon peanut oil
- 1 cup finely diced yellow onions
- 1 teaspoon paprika
- ⅛ teaspoon cayenne pepper
- ¼ teaspoon coarse sea salt
- 1 tablespoon minced fresh ginger
- 2 large cloves garlic, minced
- 2 cups peeled and finely diced yellow potato
- ½ cup peeled and finely diced carrot
- ½ cup peeled and diced parsnip
- 2 cups peeled and diced sweet potato
- 3 tablespoons creamy peanut butter
- 2 tablespoons tomato paste
- 5 cups vegetable stock, homemade (page 42) or store-bought

Freshly ground white pepper

¼ cup packed chopped flat-leaf parsley

I HAD THE IDEA *for adding dumplings to this take on peanut stew after seeing Hugh Fearnley-Whittingstall's recipe Mushroom "Stoup" in the cookbook River Cottage Veg.*

DUMPLINGS

- ½ cup whole wheat pastry flour
- ½ cup yellow cornmeal
- 2 tablespoons minced fresh thyme
- 2 teaspoons finely ground golden flaxseeds
- 1½ teaspoons baking powder
- ½ teaspoon fine sea salt
- 3 tablespoons cold plain, unsweetened soy milk
- 1 tablespoon extra-virgin olive oil

To make the stew, warm the oil in a large saucepan over medium heat. Add the onions, paprika, cayenne, and salt and sauté until the onions are soft, 5 to 7 minutes. Add the ginger, garlic, potato, carrot, parsnip, and sweet potato and sauté until the vegetables begin to soften, 5 to 7 minutes. Decrease the heat to medium-low.

Put the peanut butter, tomato paste, and 2 cups of the stock in a blender and process until smooth. Pour into the saucepan and stir in the remaining 3 cups stock. Bring to a simmer, cover partially, and cook, stirring occasionally, until the vegetables are tender, about 30 minutes.

Meanwhile, make the dumplings. Put about 5 cups of water in a medium saucepan and bring to a boil over high heat. Sift the flour, cornmeal, thyme, flaxseeds, baking powder, and salt into a medium bowl and stir with a whisk until well blended. Make a well in the center, add the soy milk and oil, and stir just until the mixture forms a batter that comes away from the sides of the bowl.

Decrease the heat under the saucepan of water to low and maintain a slow simmer. With a soup spoon, gently drop tablespoons of the batter into the water, waiting about 15 seconds before adding the next spoonful of batter. When the batter is used up, cover and simmer until the dumplings are puffed, about 10 minutes. Using a slotted spoon, gently transfer the dumplings to a plate.

Season the stew with salt and white pepper to taste. Serve each bowl of stew with a few dumplings on top. Garnish with the parsley.

STEWED TOMATOES and BLACK-EYED PEAS with CORNBREAD CROUTONS

TOMATO, CREOLE SPICE BLEND, BASIL

YIELD 4 to 6 servings

SOUNDTRACK "Back Then" by Citizen Cope from *One Lovely Day*

1½ cups dried black-eyed peas, sorted and soaked in water overnight

1 (3-inch) piece of kombu

1½ teaspoons coarse sea salt

1 tablespoon extra-virgin olive oil

½ cup finely diced yellow onion

¼ cup finely diced celery, strings removed (see sidebar, page 74)

1 clove garlic, minced

1 teaspoon Creole spice blend, homemade (page 12) or store-bought

1 (28-ounce) can plum tomatoes with juices, halved lengthwise

1 cup vegetable stock, homemade (page 42) or store-bought

1 tablespoon chopped fresh basil

2 cups Cornbread Croutons (page 132)

THERE ARE SO MANY WAYS *to enjoy black-eyed peas, but this has to be one of my favorites. The earthy flavor of the black-eyed peas and the tanginess of the tomatoes are a perfect match, which is probably why this dish is so popular in the South. The pièce de résistance of this dish, however, is the Cornbread Croutons. Their crunchy texture adds a terrific mouthfeel to each bite, and they are delicious after soaking up the tomato broth.*

Drain the black-eyed peas and rinse them well. Transfer to a medium saucepan and add the kombu and enough water to cover by 2 inches. Bring to a boil over medium heat. Decrease the heat to medium-low, skim off any foam, and partially cover. Simmer just until tender, 40 to 50 minutes. Stir in 1 teaspoon of the salt and simmer for 5 minutes. Drain well.

Meanwhile, warm the oil in a medium saucepan over medium heat. Add the onion and celery and sauté until soft, 5 to 7 minutes. Add the garlic, Creole spice blend, and the remaining ½ teaspoon salt and sauté until the garlic is fragrant, 2 to 3 minutes. In a food processor fitted with a metal blade, pulse the tomatoes with their juice until coarsely chopped. Add the chopped tomatoes, the stock, and the black-eyed peas to the saucepan, stir, and bring to a simmer. Decrease the heat to medium-low, cover, and simmer, stirring occasionally, until thickening, about 45 minutes. Stir in the basil and cook for 1 minute more. Taste and season with more salt if desired. Serve topped with the croutons.

TOFU CURRY with MUSTARD GREENS

MUSTARD SEEDS, TURMERIC, CUMIN, CARDAMOM, CHILI POWDER, GINGER

YIELD 4 to 6 servings	**SOUNDTRACK** "Green Chimneys" by Thelonious Monk from *Underground*

- 14 to 16 ounces extra-firm tofu, cut into ½-inch cubes
- 3 tablespoons plus 2 teaspoons extra-virgin olive oil
- ¾ teaspoon fine sea salt
- ¼ teaspoon mustard seeds
- 1 cup finely diced white onion
- 2 cloves garlic, minced
- 1 tablespoon minced fresh ginger
- 1½ teaspoons ground turmeric
- ½ teaspoon cumin seeds, toasted (see sidebar, page 9) and ground
- 6 cardamom pods, toasted (see sidebar, page 9), then seeds removed and ground
- ½ teaspoon chili powder
- ¼ teaspoon freshly ground black pepper
- ¼ teaspoon garlic powder
- ¼ teaspoon ground ginger
- 1 (14-ounce) can chopped tomatoes with juices
- 1 heaping tablespoon chunky peanut butter
- 1 jalapeño chile, seeded and minced
- 3 cups vegetable stock, homemade (page 42) or store-bought
- 12 ounces mustard greens, stemmed and cut into bite-size pieces
- 2 bay leaves
- 2 tablespoons chopped cilantro

I WAS INSPIRED *to make this dish after seeing a recipe for Tanzanian fish curry in* The Taste of Africa, *by Rosamund Grant and Josephine Bacon. My version is pretty straightforward: the tofu makes it hearty and satisfying, the greens are tender and give the dish a nourishing feel, and the curried broth brings everything together.*

Preheat the oven to 450°F. Line a rimmed baking sheet with parchment paper.

Put the tofu in a bowl, drizzle with 2 teaspoons of the oil, and sprinkle with ¼ teaspoon of the salt. Gently toss the tofu with clean hands until evenly coated. Transfer to the lined baking sheet, spreading the tofu in a single layer. Bake, turning once after 15 minutes, for 30 mintues, until firm.

Meanwhile, warm the remaining 3 tablespoons oil in a large sauté pan over medium heat. Add the mustard seeds and cook, shaking the pan occasionally, until they pop, 2 to 3 minutes. Add the onion and the remaining ½ teaspoon salt and sauté until soft, 5 to 7 minutes. Add the garlic, fresh ginger, turmeric, cumin, cardamom, chili powder, black pepper, garlic powder, and ground ginger and sauté until fragrant, about 2 minutes. Add the tomatoes, peanut butter, and jalapeño and stir until well combined. Stir in the stock, mustard greens, and bay leaves and bring to a simmer. Decrease the heat to medium-low, partially cover, and simmer, stirring occasionally, for 20 minutes.

Gently stir in the tofu and cook for 10 minutes. Remove the bay leaves. Taste and season with more salt and black pepper if desired. Serve garnished with the cilantro.

SWEET POTATO and LIMA BEAN TAGINE

SAFFRON, GINGER, CINNAMON, CILANTRO

YIELD 4 to 6 servings || **SOUNDTRACK** "Ya Messinagh" by Tinariwen (featuring The Dirty Dozen Brass Band) from *Tassili*

⅔ cup dried lima beans, sorted and soaked in water overnight

1 (3-inch) piece of kombu

1½ teaspoons coarse sea salt

Scant 2 cups vegetable stock, homemade (page 42) or store-bought

Large pinch of saffron threads

2 tablespoons extra-virgin olive oil

1 cup finely diced yellow onion

2 large cloves garlic, minced

1 tablespoon minced fresh ginger

2 pounds sweet potatoes, peeled and cut into ½-inch cubes

1 teaspoon agave nectar

1 (2-inch) cinnamon stick

Freshly ground white pepper

¼ cup packed chopped cilantro

Spicy Mustard Greens (page 25), for serving

TAGINE, A POPULAR DISH in North Africa, is named after the earthenware pot in which these stews are traditionally cooked. This is a simple version that combines ingredients from the American South with herbs and spices used in traditional North African cooking. Like most stews, this dish tastes even better after the flavors have melded overnight. Serve it with Skillet Cornbread with Pecan Dukkah (page 131) for a satisfying meal.

Drain the lima beans and rinse them well. Transfer to a medium saucepan and add the kombu and enough water to cover by 2 inches. Bring to a boil over high heat. Decrease the heat to medium-low, partially cover, and simmer until just tender but still firm, 25 to 45 minutes. Check the beans often to ensure that they don't overcook, skimming off any foam and discarding any floating skins. Stir in 1 teaspoon of the salt and simmer for 5 minutes. Drain in a colander, remove the kombu, and rinse the beans under cold water.

Pour the stock into a medium bowl and crumble the saffron into it.

Warm the oil in a large pot over medium heat. Add the onion and sauté until soft, 3 to 5 minutes. Add the garlic, ginger, and the remaining ½ teaspoon salt and sauté until fragrant, 2 to 3 minutes. Pour in the stock. Add the sweet potatoes, agave nectar, and cinnamon stick and bring to a boil. Decrease the heat to low, cover, and simmer, stirring occasionally, for 20 minutes.

Stir in the lima beans and cook, stirring occasionally, until the sweet potatoes are fork-tender, about 10 minutes. Discard the cinnamon stick. Season with white pepper and, if desired, more salt. Serve garnished with the cilantro and offer the harissa alongside.

GREENS. SQUASHES. ROOTS.

PLANT-FOCUSED MEALS ARE NOTHING NEW to traditional African and Caribbean diets, and prior to the industrialization of U.S. food, even the oft-maligned diet of African-Americans in the Southern states placed a heavy emphasis on locally grown vegetables. This chapter not only honors the diverse leafy greens, pumpkins, squashes, roots, and other vegetables common to all cuisines of the African diaspora, but also highlights the historically rich bounty that I enjoyed while growing up in Memphis, Tennessee. Many recipes are simple uncooked salads or light sautés. Others offer a delightful spin on classic dishes from different regions. All celebrate the exciting range of flavors and textures possible in a plant-based diet.

There were a number of African and Caribbean vegetables that I wanted to present in this book, but I have stuck to ones that can be easily found in the United States. Similar to the way that enslaved Africans had to create imaginative culinary traditions using foods in the New World that resembled those of their homeland (for example, replacing the yams of Africa with the sweet potatoes of the South), I use comparable ingredients that honor the flavors and spirit of the original dish. For example, I pay homage to *ndolé*, the national dish of Cameroon, by replacing West African bitter leaves with fresh spinach. Other dishes fuse distinctive sauces found in countries throughout Africa with ingredients indigenous to North America (see Grilled Corn on the Cob, page 64). For several recipes, I draw on the memory of vegetables from my childhood or the bounty pulled from my home garden and prepare them simply for a light and clean dish that respects the current season, such as the Sautéed Sugar Snap Peas with Spring Herbs (page 60) and the All-Green Spring Slaw (page 74).

SAUTÉED SUGAR SNAP PEAS with SPRING HERBS

OLIVE OIL, LEMON JUICE, ORANGE ZEST, PARSLEY, CILANTRO, CHIVES, SESAME SEEDS

YIELD 4 to 6 servings | **SOUNDTRACK** "United" by Art Blakey & The Jazz Messengers from *Roots & Herbs*

2 teaspoons chopped fresh chives

1 teaspoon minced flat-leaf parsley

1 teaspoon minced cilantro

1½ teaspoons coarse sea salt

1½ pound sugar snap peas, trimmed

1 tablespoon extra-virgin olive oil

1 large clove garlic, minced

2 teaspoons finely grated orange zest

1 teaspoon freshly squeezed lemon juice

Freshly ground white pepper

1 teaspoon black sesame seeds, toasted (see sidebar, page 119)

WHEN MY PAW PAW *cooked sugar snap peas he grew in his garden, he always prepared them simply, with a little butter. I like to eat mine with lots of spring herbs after a quick sauté in olive oil.*

Put the chives, parsley, and cilantro in a small bowl and mix well.

Put about 12 cups of water in a large pot and bring to a boil over high heat. Add 1 teaspoon of the salt, then add the sugar snap peas and blanch for 30 seconds. Drain well.

Heat the oil in a large skillet over medium heat. Add the garlic and sauté until fragrant, 2 to 3 minutes. Add the peas and the remaining ½ teaspoon salt, increase the heat to high, and cook, shaking the pan and tossing vigorously, for about 1 minute. Transfer to a large bowl, add the orange zest and lemon juice, and toss until the peas are evenly coated. Serve topped with the chive mixture, a few grinds of white pepper, and the sesame seeds.

MUSCOVADO-ROASTED PLANTAINS

OLIVE OIL, MAPLE SYRUP

YIELD 4 to 6 servings | **SOUNDTRACK** "Golden Lady" by José Feliciano from *And the Feeling's Good*

4 large ripe plantains, ends cut off, peeled, and cut into thirds

4 teaspoons olive oil

½ teaspoon coarse sea salt

1 tablespoon maple syrup

¼ cup muscovado sugar

INSPIRED BY *candied sweet potatoes, this flavorfully sweet side dish provides a satisfying counterpoint to a savory main. While roasting brings out the natural sweetness in plantains, muscovado—unrefined brown cane sugar—gives the plantains a subtle molasses flavor. You can add chopped pecans for texture. If you cannot find muscovado, use raw cane sugar and replace the maple syrup with 1 teaspoon unsulfured molasses.*

Preheat the oven to 375°F. Line a large, rimmed baking sheet with parchment paper.

Put the plantains in a large bowl, drizzle with 2 teaspoons of the oil, and sprinkle with the salt. Toss gently until the plantains are evenly coated. Transfer to the lined baking sheet and bake for 40 minutes, gently stirring and turning every 10 minutes, until fork-tender and lightly browned.

Combine the maple syrup, muscovado, and remaining 2 teaspoons oil in a small bowl and stir with a fork to combine. Pour into a large skillet and warm over high heat until melted, about 30 seconds. Add the plantains, and cook for 1 minute, tossing vigorously to coat evenly, and serve.

HEIRLOOM TOMATO SALAD
and BASIL SEA SALT

OLIVE OIL, BLACK PEPPER

YIELD
4 servings

SOUNDTRACK "Summertime" by Angélique Kidjo from *Keep On Moving: The Best of Angélique Kidjo*

2 pounds heirloom tomatoes of varying shapes, sizes, and colors

Best-quality extra-virgin olive oil, for drizzling

Basil Salt (page 13)

Freshly ground black pepper

IN AUGUST, *heirloom tomatoes are at their peak, and you should be able to find them at your local farmers' market, some natural food stores, and, increasingly, at conventional supermarkets.*

Cut the tomatoes in various styles—a mix of halves, quarters, and slices—to enhance presentation.

Divide the tomatoes evenly among 4 plates, drizzle with oil, and sprinkle with Basil Salt and black pepper to taste.

GRILLED CORN ON THE COB

SWEET CORN, SEA SALT, BLACK PEPPER

YIELD 4 to 6 servings

SOUNDTRACK "Prophecies" by Audiopharmacy from *Spare Change*

6 ears of sweet corn

2 tablespoons coarse sea salt

¼ cup Smoky Pili Pili Sauce (page 23) or Spicy Mustard Greens (page 25)

Freshly ground black pepper

ONE OF MY FAVORITE *ways to eat grilled corn on the cob is coated with a mixture of olive oil and green Tabasco sauce, and I thought tangy Smoky Pili Pili Sauce would be equally satisfying. I was right! For a different twist, slather on Spicy Mustard Greens (page 25).*

Peel back the corn husks but leave them attached. Remove the corn silk, then wrap the husks back around the corn. Put the corn in a large pot and add the salt. Put a plate on the corn to weight it, then add cold water to cover the corn. Let soak for at least 2 hours.

Prepare a medium-high grill. Drain the corn. If necessary, tie the tops of the corn husks with kitchen twine to keep them closed.

Put the corn on the grill, cover, and cook, turning occasionally with tongs, until the husks are slightly charred and the kernels are tender, about 25 minutes. Let the ears cool until they can be handled, then fold back the husks.

Pour a little sauce over each ear, then, using your hands, rub the sauce evenly over the corn. Season with a few grinds of pepper and serve immediately.

---

raw alternative | FRESH CORN SALAD with BELL PEPPERS and TOMATOES

YIELD 4 servings

Kernels from 4 ears of sweet corn (store the cobs in the freezer to make Corn Broth, page 43)

½ cup finely diced green bell pepper

1 cup finely diced seeded heirloom tomato

2 teaspoons extra-virgin olive oil

1 African bird's eye chile, minced

½ teaspoon coarse sea salt

Freshly ground white pepper

⅓ cup very thinly sliced fresh basil

When summer vegetables are at their freshest, I like to let them shine without interfering too much. This salad should be made with the freshest sweet corn, the crunchiest bell peppers, and the juiciest heirloom tomatoes that you can find. You could sauté this mixture in olive oil, too.

Combine the corn, bell pepper, tomato, oil, chile, and salt in a medium bowl and stir to combine. Season with white pepper and, if desired, more salt. Serve garnished with the basil.

MILLET-and-PEANUT-STUFFED AVOCADO with HARISSA SALSA

TOMATO, GREEN BELL PEPPER

YIELD	SOUNDTRACK "Patta Patta Boota Boota" by Mehdi Hassan from *Music of Pakistan - Ghazals, Volume 2*
4 servings	

HARISSA SALSA

- 2 cups finely diced tomatoes
- 2 teaspoons coconut oil
- 2 tablespoons Harissa (page 24)
- 1 teaspoon coriander seeds, toasted (see sidebar, page 9) and ground
- 1 teaspoon coarse sea salt
- ½ teaspoon chili powder

MILLET

- 2 cups water
- 1 cup millet
- 2 tablespoons coconut oil
- ½ cup diced red onion
- ½ cup diced green bell pepper
- 1 tablespoon minced garlic
- ½ cup unsalted dry-roasted peanuts
- ¾ cup diced tomato
- 2 tablespoons freshly squeezed lemon juice
- 1 tablespoon tamari
- 1 tablespoon chili powder
- 1½ teaspoons coarse sea salt
- 1½ teaspoons smoked paprika

- 4 large avocados
- ½ cup minced cilantro, for garnish

MY BUDDY AYINDE HOWELL *is one of my favorite vegan chefs, so I invited him to contribute this recipe. In addition to doing pop-up dinners across the country and serving as India Arie's personal chef, Ayinde is the founder of the wildly popular website ieatgrass.com. I am expecting really big things from him over the next few years, so be on the lookout.*

To make the salsa, put the tomatoes, oil, Harissa, coriander, salt, and chili powder in a blender and pulse until chunky. If you like your salsa spicier, add more Harissa.

To make the millet, in a small saucepan, bring the water and millet to a boil over high heat. Decrease the heat to medium-low and cook until the water is absorbed and the millet is fluffy, about 20 minutes. Remove from the heat and let steam, covered, for 15 minutes.

Once the millet is done steaming, heat the oil in a medium skillet over medium-high heat. Add the onion, bell pepper, and garlic and sauté until fragrant, about 3 minutes. Add the peanuts and sauté for an additional minute. Add the cooked millet and mix well, then stir in the tomato. Add the lemon juice, tamari, chili powder, 1 teaspoon of the salt, and the paprika. Decrease the heat to low and stir until warmed through, 3 to 5 minutes.

Cut the avocados in half and remove the pits. Using a large spoon, scoop the meat from each avocado half into a bowl. Sprinkle with the remaining ½ teaspoon salt, mash with a fork, and gently stir to combine.

To serve, spoon enough of the mashed avocado mixture into each avocado shell to fill halfway, reserving any remaining avocado mixture for another use. Top each avocado shell with about 5 heaping tablespoons of the millet mixture. To serve, spoon 2 to 3 generous tablespoons of the salsa over each avocado half and garnish with cilantro.

TOMATO, ONION, and CHILE PEPPER SALAD

CILANTRO, PARSLEY, LEMON JUICE, APPLE CIDER VINEGAR

YIELD 4 to 6 servings | **SOUNDTRACK** "1er Gaou" by Magic System from *Premier Gaou* | **BOOK** *Teeth* by Aracelis Girmay

2 large ripe heirloom tomatoes, seeded and finely diced

½ cup finely diced white onion

½ large jalapeño chile, seeded and minced

1 tablespoon chopped cilantro

1 tablespoon chopped flat-leaf parsley

2 teaspoons freshly squeezed lemon juice

1 teaspoon apple cider vinegar

¼ teaspoon coarse sea salt

THIS DISH IS INSPIRED BY kachumbari, *a mixture of fresh tomato and onion eaten as a side dish in East, Central, and southern Africa. It's often served as an accompaniment to spicy dishes as a cooling counterpoint. This one calls for seeded jalapeño to make it interesting, but you can omit the chile if you want to keep your version completely cool. This recipe makes a small quantity because it's intended as a condiment, but feel free to double the recipe.*

Put all the ingredients in a large bowl and toss gently to combine. Refrigerate until chilled, at least 1 hour. Serve cold.

INSPIRING AND EDUCATIONAL ART

Much of the suggested cultural matter in this book is meant to inspire and educate. Art, music, literature, and film have had a powerful impact on my development as a person, and they've played a crucial role in my thoughts around health, food, and agricultural issues. When I was a teenager, the song "Beef," a brilliant articulation of the negative impact of factory farming on animals reared for human consumption by pioneering hip-hop group Boogie Down Productions, radically shifted my thoughts around the way we treat animals. Reading about Dick Gregory's personal journey with food in his book, *Natural Diet for Folks Who Eat: Cookin' with Mother Nature*, moved me to experiment with various health-supportive models of eating, such as vegetarianism, veganism, raw foodism, and frutarianism. Watching *Life and Debt*, a documentary film about the negative impact of economic globalization on Jamaica's agricultural system, played a major role in influencing me to start b-healthy, an organization that taught young people to cook and equipped them to be educators and organizers around food issues in their communities.

CITRUS SALAD with ARUGULA

NAVEL ORANGE, GRAPEFRUIT, ARUGULA, CILANTRO

YIELD 4 to 6 servings | **SOUNDTRACK** "Malemolência" (1000 Grau Martins Remix) by Céu from *Remixed EP*

2 large pink grapefruits

8 large navel oranges

2 tablespoons minced cilantro

½ teaspoon coarse sea salt

Freshly ground white pepper

2 tablespoons extra-virgin olive oil

3 cups packed baby arugula

THIS REFRESHING SALAD *is inspired by the fresh orange slices that are often served with the popular Brazilian bean stew feijoada. If you serve it as an accompaniment to Black Bean and Seitan Stew (page 50), you can't go wrong. In fact, it would work well as a final course in any heavy meal. This salad is best during the cooler winter months, when citrus season is at its peak. Experiment with other citrus fruits, such as blood oranges, clementines, satsumas, and tangerines.*

With a sharp knife, remove the rind and bitter white pith from 1 grapefruit. Holding the fruit over a large bowl to catch the juices and sections, cut just inside the membrane of each section and loosen until it falls into the bowl. With a slotted spoon, transfer the grapefruit sections to a clean bowl and discard any seeds. Repeat with the remaining grapefruit sections and with the oranges, adding the sections to the bowl with the grapefruit.

Arrange the grapefruit and orange sections over three-fourths of a serving plate and set aside. Strain the juices and put 3 tablespoons of the juice in a blender. (Drink any remaining juice or reserve it for another use.) Add the cilantro, salt, a few grinds of pepper, and the oil and process until creamy.

Put the arugula in the bowl that held the juices and pour in just enough dressing to coat lightly, reserving the remaining dressing for another use. Toss with clean hands, then mound the arugula in the empty area of the serving plate. Serve immediately.

SUMMER VEGETABLE and TOFU KEBABS with POMEGRANATE-PEACH BARBECUE SAUCE

POTATO, EGGPLANT, BELL PEPPER, RED ONION

YIELD
5 servings

SOUNDTRACK "When You're a Rose (Revisited)" by Grey Reverend from *Everlasting EP*

28 ounces extra-firm tofu, frozen and thawed

5 cups Pomegranate-Peach Barbecue Sauce (page 18)

4 ounces small round potatoes, halved

3 tablespoons extra-virgin olive oil, plus more for oiling

1 tablespoon freshly squeezed lemon juice

1 large clove garlic, minced

1 teaspoon coarse sea salt

Pinch of cayenne pepper

1 globe eggplant (about 1 pound), cut into 1-inch chunks

1 green bell pepper, cut into 1-inch squares

1 large red bell pepper, cut into 1-inch squares

1 large red onion, quartered vertically, then halved crosswise

YOU CAN'T GO WRONG serving these kebabs at a cookout. You can prepare them in advance, and they're practically a meal unto themselves when served along with couscous, potato salad, or a grain-based dish. And what a great way to showcase summer's bounty of vegetables! Tweak the recipe by using whatever vegetables are most exciting to you. Note that this recipe requires a fair amount of advance preparation: freezing and then thawing the tofu, marinating the thawed tofu overnight, and preparing a double batch of the barbecue sauce.

Put the tofu on a plate. Put another plate on top and weight it (a 28-ounce can of tomatoes works well) to press the excess moisture out of the tofu. Let sit for at least 20 minutes. Drain away the liquid and cut the tofu into 1/2-inch cubes. Put the tofu and 2 cups of the barbecue sauce in a large bowl and toss gently until the tofu is evenly coated. Transfer all the contents of the bowl to a ziplock bag and refrigerate overnight.

Remove the tofu from the refrigerator and let it warm to room temperature. Put the potatoes in a small saucepan, add water to cover, and bring to a boil over high heat. Decrease the heat to medium-low, cover, and cook until just fork-tender, 8 to 10 minutes. Drain and let cool.

Prepare a medium-high grill. While the grill is heating, put the oil, lemon juice, garlic, salt, and cayenne in a large bowl and whisk to combine. Add the potatoes, eggplant, green and red bell peppers, and onion and toss gently until evenly coated.

Next, thread the tofu and vegetables onto 10 metal skewers, distributing them evenly among the skewers. Put the remaining 3 cups barbecue sauce in a small saucepan and add any sauce remaining in the ziplock bag. Bring to a boil over high heat, stirring frequently, and continue cooking for about 1 minute. Transfer to a serving bowl.

Brush the grill grate with oil. Put the kebabs on the grill and cook, turning frequently, until the tofu is lightly charred and the vegetables are fork-tender, about 8 minutes. Serve with the hot barbecue sauce alongside.

ALL-GREEN SPRING SLAW

GREEN CABBAGE, GREEN PEAS, SUGAR SNAP PEAS, CELERY, PUMPKIN SEEDS, PARSLEY, CHIVES

YIELD 4 to 6 servings | **SOUNDTRACK** "Mobius Streak" by Hiatus Kaiyote (Dufrane Remix) from *TAWK TAKEOUT* (*Tawk Tomahawk Remixed*)

DRESSING

- ¼ cup silken tofu
- 1 tablespoon freshly squeezed lemon juice
- 1 tablespoon Dijon mustard
- 2 tablespoons apple cider vinegar
- 1 clove garlic, minced
- ½ teaspoon coarse sea salt
- 2 tablespoons extra-virgin olive oil

SLAW

- 3 cups very thinly sliced green cabbage
- 2 teaspoons coarse sea salt
- ½ cup shelled green peas (about 8 ounces peas in the pod)
- 8 ounces sugar snap peas, trimmed and thinly sliced lengthwise
- 2 stalks celery, strings removed and thinly sliced diagonally (see sidebar)
- ¼ cup husked raw pumpkin seeds, toasted (see sidebar, page 119)
- ½ cup packed chopped flat-leaf parsley
- 2 tablespoons chopped fresh chives
- 1 tablespoon finely grated lime zest

THIS DISH IS MY MODERN take on classic coleslaw. *The delicate flavor of the green peas and sugar snap peas make this an exceptional dish, and the crunch from the celery and pumpkin seeds is extremely satisfying. The tangy dressing is top-notch too, so reserve any extra to use on another salad.*

To make the dressing, put the tofu, lemon juice, mustard, vinegar, garlic, and salt in a blender and process until somewhat mixed. With the motor running, slowly pour in the oil and process until creamy. Taste and season with more salt if desired.

To make the slaw, put the cabbage in a large bowl and sprinkle with the salt. With clean hands, massage the cabbage until soft and wilted, about 3 minutes. Transfer to a colander and rinse the bowl. Put the colander in the sink, put a plate atop the cabbage, and weight it (a 28-ounce can of tomatoes works well). Let sit for 1 hour.

Rinse the cabbage under cold water, then squeeze with clean hands to extract as much liquid as possible. Return the cabbage to the large bowl and add the shelled peas, sugar snap peas, celery, and pumpkin seeds. Pour in enough dressing to lightly coat the vegetables (start with 3 tablespoons). Toss with clean hands, then taste and add more dressing as desired (reserve any extra for another use).

To serve, with clean hands, transfer the slaw to a serving bowl, leaving any juices behind. Garnish with the parsley, chives, and lime zest.

HOW TO REMOVE TOUGH STRINGS FROM CELERY

I find that the strings in celery stalks make the celery hard to chew, so I usually take them off. I typically use a vegetable peeler to lightly remove the top layer, getting rid of all the strings.

BLACKENED CAULIFLOWER
with PLUM TOMATO SAUCE

OLIVE OIL, BLACKENED SEASONING, THYME

YIELD	**SOUNDTRACK** "Putting Up Resistance" by Beres Hammond from *Putting Up* Resistance
6 servings	

SAUCE

2 tablespoons extra-virgin olive oil

1 large clove garlic, minced

½ teaspoon coarse sea salt

1 (28-ounce) can plum tomatoes with juices, chopped

½ teaspoon red wine vinegar

Freshly ground white pepper

CAULIFLOWER

2 pounds cauliflower, trimmed

1 tablespoon coarse sea salt

Extra-virgin olive oil, for brushing

¼ cup blackened seasoning, homemade (page 9) or store-bought

2 tablespoons minced fresh thyme

GROWING CAULIFLOWER in our home garden has completely shifted my thoughts about how flavorful this cruciferous vegetable can be. Fresh out of a garden, you don't need to do much more than blanch and season it with a little oil, salt, and pepper. Fully aware that most store-bought cauliflower lacks deep flavor and inspired by the recent trend of cooking cauliflower "steaks" as a hearty centerpiece to vegetarian and vegan meals, I created this recipe. After blanching thickly cut slices of cauliflower and coating them with my Blackened Seasoning, I cook them using the "blackening" technique often associated with Cajun cuisine. The result is a richly flavored, hearty dish that I often top with tempeh, tofu, or beans. Here I top the cauliflower with a simple tomato sauce; you could top it with Tomato, Onion, and Chile Pepper Salad (page 69) during the summer for a lighter dish. You can also cover it with Chermoula Tempeh Bites (page 116) for an exciting entrée. Note: make sure that your kitchen is well ventilated, since this cooking technique produces a lot of smoke.

To make the sauce, warm the oil in a medium saucepan over medium heat. Add the garlic and salt and sauté until the garlic is fragrant, about 3 minutes. Stir in the tomatoes and their juices, increase the heat to high, and bring to a boil. Decrease the heat to medium-low, partially cover, and simmer, stirring occasionally, for 15 minutes. Stir in the vinegar and cook for 1 more minute. Season with salt and white pepper to taste. Cover and set aside.

To prepare the cauliflower, preheat the oven to 400°F and line a baking sheet with parchment paper.

Using a sharp chef's knife, cut each head of cauliflower into three 3/4-inch-thick slices, reserving the remaining cauliflower for another use. Put about 4 quarts of water in a large pot and bring to a boil over high heat. Add the salt, then, with tongs, gently lower 3 of the cauliflower slices into the water, one at a time. Cover and cook for 2 1/2 minutes. Gently transfer to a colander to drain. Repeat with the remaining cauliflower. Arrange the cauliflower slices on the prepared baking sheet (or 2 baking sheets if need be) and bake for about 16 minutes, until fork-tender.

Brush both sides of the cauliflower slices with oil and sprinkle with the blackened seasoning. Warm a large, dry cast-iron skillet over high heat. Put a slice of cauliflower in the skillet and cook, without disturbing, until starting to crisp on the bottom, about 1 1/2 minutes. With a spatula, gently turn and fry until the other side is starting to crisp, about 1 1/2 minutes. Repeat with the remaining slices.

To serve, quickly reheat the tomato sauce and top each slice with a generous spoonful. Garnish with the thyme.

COLLARDS and CABBAGE with LOTS OF GARLIC

COLLARD GREENS, SAVOY CABBAGE, OLIVE OIL, GARLIC, SEA SALT

YIELD 4 to 6 servings

SOUNDTRACK "Cassius Marcelo Clay" by Jorge Ben from *Negro É Lindo*

8 ounces Savoy cabbage, cored

12 ounces collard greens, stemmed

1 tablespoon plus ½ teaspoon coarse sea salt

2 tablespoons extra-virgin olive oil

7 cloves garlic, thinly sliced

¼ cup vegetable stock, homemade (page 42) or store-bought, or water

THIS IS A SIMPLE SIDE *that could work with almost any fall or winter meal. It mashes up Monrovian collard greens and cabbage (a Liberian dish) with couve à mineira (Brazilian collard greens). The key is to cut the cabbage and collards as thinly as possible (I mean thread thin) to help lighten up their earthy flavor.*

Put about 12 cups of water in a large pot over high heat and bring to a boil. While the water is heating up, cut the cabbage into paper-thin strips and set aside. Stack 4 collard leaves on top of one another, roll up lengthwise into a tight cylinder, and slice crosswise into paper-thin strips. Repeat with the remaining collard leaves.

When the water is boiling, add 1 tablespoon of the salt, then gently lower the cabbage into the water. Return to a boil and cook uncovered until just wilted, about 30 seconds. Using a slotted spoon, transfer the cabbage to a colander to drain. Next, gently lower the collard greens into the boiling water. Return to a boil and cook uncovered until soft, 8 to 10 minutes. Transfer the cabbage to a bowl, then drain the collard greens in the colander.

Warm the oil in a large sauté pan over medium heat. Add the garlic and the remaining ½ teaspoon salt and sauté until the garlic just starts to turn golden, about 5 minutes. Add the collard greens and sauté for 2 minutes. Stir in the cabbage and sauté until tender, about 4 minutes. Stir in the stock, cover, and cook until most of the liquid has evaporated, about 3 minutes. Serve hot.

DANDELION SALAD with PECAN DRESSING

TANGERINE, PECANS, CILANTRO

YIELD 4 to 6 servings

SOUNDTRACK "Down in Memphis" by Booker T. Jones from *The Road from Memphis*

BOOK *When the Only Light Is Fire* by Saeed Jones

DRESSING

6 tablespoons finely chopped pecans

6 tablespoons freshly squeezed orange juice

2 teaspoons freshly squeezed lemon juice

1 teaspoon Dijon mustard

¼ cup packed cilantro leaves

¼ teaspoon coarse sea salt

2 tablespoons extra-virgin olive oil

SALAD

7 large tangerines

6 cups torn stemmed dandelion greens

¾ cup chopped Sugared Pecans (page 119)

Freshly ground black pepper

WHILE THEY ARE NOT *often associated with Southern foodways in the popular imagination, dandelion greens are a staple in traditional African-American cooking. My family grew them, and we cooked them along with collard and mustard greens and other leafy vegetables. They are often used as a healing and preventative herb during the spring when they're at their peak, and they're a good source of vitamins A, B6, K, and E, as well as thiamin, riboflavin, calcium, iron, copper, and potassium. Tangerines, which are cultivated in Algeria, add a sweet counterpoint to the bitterness from the dandelion greens in this salad, and the sugar-coated pecans add sweet crunch.*

To make the dressing, combine the pecans, orange juice, lemon juice, mustard, cilantro, and salt in a blender and process until smooth. With the motor running, slowly pour in the oil and process until creamy. Taste and season with more salt if desired.

To make the salad, use a sharp knife to remove the rind and bitter white pith from 1 tangerine. Holding the fruit over a large bowl to catch the juices and sections, cut just inside the membrane of each section and loosen until it falls into the bowl. Discard any seeds. Repeat with the remaining tangerines.

Add the dandelion greens and pecans. Pour in enough dressing to lightly coat the salad, saving any remaining dressing for another use, and gently toss. Season each serving with a few grinds of black pepper.

QUICK-PICKLED VEGETABLE SALAD

GREEN CABBAGE, CARROT, VIDALIA ONION, AFRICAN BIRD'S EYE CHILE

YIELD 4 to 6 servings

SOUNDTRACK "Green Power" by Quasimoto from *The Unseen*

1½ pounds green cabbage, very thinly sliced

2¼ teaspoons coarse sea salt

1 cup rice vinegar

1 cup water

2 tablespoons raw cane sugar

1 teaspoon black peppercorns

1 large carrot, cut into ribbons with a vegetable peeler

½ cup very thinly sliced Vidalia onion, in rings

2 African bird's eye chiles, thinly sliced

2 tablespoons chopped flat-leaf parsley

2 tablespoons chopped cilantro

INSPIRED BY THE CABBAGE-BASED SIDE SALAD commonly eaten throughout eastern Africa, this tangy and intense salad goes well with richly flavored main dishes. It would taste good on Berbere-Spiced Black-Eyed Pea Sliders (page 32) or any other sandwich that needs crunch and zing. It could also be served alongside Chermoula Tempeh Bites (page 116) to provide a sweet, sour, and spicy contrast.

Put the cabbage in a large bowl and sprinkle with 2 teaspoons of the salt. With clean hands, massage the cabbage until soft and wilted, about 3 minutes. Transfer to a colander and rinse the bowl. Put the colander in the sink, put a plate atop the cabbage, and weight it (a 28-ounce can of tomatoes works well). Let sit for 1 hour.

Meanwhile, put the vinegar, water, sugar, peppercorns, and the remaining ¼ teaspoon salt in a medium saucepan. Cook over low heat, stirring frequently, until the sugar is completely dissolved, about 3 minutes. Remove from the heat and let cool completely.

Rinse the cabbage under cold water, then squeeze with clean hands to extract as much liquid as possible. Return the cabbage to the large bowl and add the carrot, onion, and chiles. Pour in the vinegar mixture, set the plate and weight on top, and let sit for 1 hour.

Before serving, drain the vegetables and put them in a serving bowl. Add the parsley and cilantro and toss to combine.

SLOW-BRAISED MUSTARD GREENS

GARLIC, YELLOW ONION, RAW CANE SUGAR, TOMATO PASTE, HOT-PEPPER VINEGAR

YIELD 4 to 6 servings | **SOUNDTRACK** "Slow Drag" by Donald Byrd from *Slow Drag* | **BOOK** *Long Division* by Kiese Laymon

GREENS

1 tablespoon plus ½ teaspoon coarse sea salt

1 pound mustard greens, stems and leaves chopped separately

1 tablespoon extra-virgin olive oil

1 large clove garlic, minced

4 cups vegetable stock, homemade (page 42) or store-bought

ONIONS

3 tablespoons extra-virgin olive oil

3 large yellow onions, sliced into thin rings

2 teaspoons raw cane sugar

6 tablespoons tomato paste

1 tablespoon water

1 jalapeño chile, seeded and minced

Hot-pepper vinegar, homemade (page 20) or store-bought, for serving

THIS IS PROBABLY MY FAVORITE *recipe in this book. I was so proud of myself for transforming a mundane side dish, braised greens, into a complexly flavored and delicious standout. Inspired by* smoor *tomatoes and onions—a traditional South African dish eaten as a sauce, relish, or side—I caramelize onions, then sauté them with tomato paste. I top slow-braised mustard greens with this mixture and finish it with minced jalapeños and hot-pepper vinegar. Warm, savory, and tangy sweet, this dish is everything a side of greens in pot likker should be.*

To prepare the greens, put about 12 cups of water in a large pot and bring to a boil over high heat. Add the 1 tablespoon of the salt, then add the greens and their stems and cook uncovered until soft, about 5 minutes. Drain well.

Warm the oil in a large sauté pan over medium heat. Add the garlic and the remaining ½ teaspoon salt and sauté until the garlic is fragrant, about 3 minutes. Stir in the greens and stock, increase the heat to high, and bring to a boil. Decrease the heat to low, cover, and simmer until meltingly tender, about 45 minutes.

Meanwhile, prepare the onions. Warm the oil in a separate large sauté pan over medium-low heat. Add the onions and sugar and sauté until deep golden brown and quite soft, about 15 minutes. Stir in the tomato paste and water and cook, stirring often, until the onions are thoroughly coated and hot, about 3 minutes.

To serve, portion the greens along with some of their liquid into small bowls. Top with the onions, sprinkle with the jalapeño, and drizzle some hot-pepper vinegar on top.

SPINACH-PEANUT SAUCE

SPINACH, PEANUTS, ONION, GARLIC, GINGER

YIELD
4 cups

SOUNDTRACK "Kurumalete" by Richard Bona from *The Ten Shades of Blues*

2 tablespoons extra-virgin olive oil

1½ cups finely diced yellow onion

1 tablespoon minced fresh ginger

½ teaspoon coarse sea salt

2 large cloves garlic, minced

1½ pounds spinach leaves (about 12 packed cups)

½ cup skinless raw peanuts, soaked in water overnight and drained

3 cups vegetable stock, homemade (page 42) or store-bought

1 teaspoon minced fresh thyme

THIS RICHLY FLAVORED *combination of spinach and peanuts is inspired by ndolé, the national dish of Cameroon. I first learned about it from my buddy Malong Pendar, who is the owner and executive chef of A Taste of Africa, an African food truck/pop-up restaurant in Oakland, California. His veggie combo plates are divine, and they always include a generous helping of ndolé poured over rice. I imagine this dish being eaten similarly, along with greens and plantains.*

Heat the oil in a medium sauté pan over medium heat. Add the onion, ginger, and salt and sauté until the onion is soft and translucent, about 10 minutes. Add the garlic and sauté until fragrant, 2 to 3 minutes. Remove from the heat.

Put the spinach in a large sauté pan over medium-high heat and add about 2 cups of water. Cover and cook, stirring a few times, until the spinach wilts, about 5 minutes. Drain well, pressing the spinach to extract as much liquid as possible.

When cool enough to handle, transfer to a cutting board and chop finely. Add the spinach to the onion.

Put the peanuts and stock in a blender and process until smooth. Transfer to the pan with the onion. Cover and cook over low heat, stirring often, until the sauce is thick, about 45 minutes. Stir in the thyme and cook for 2 to 3 minutes. Taste and season with more salt if desired. Serve hot.

GRILLED ZUCCHINI with MIXED-HERB MARINADE

OLIVE OIL, LEMON JUICE, ORANGE JUICE, GARLIC, PARSLEY, THYME, CHERVIL

YIELD 4 to 6 servings

SOUNDTRACK "Rak El Habib" by Oum Kulthum from *Rak El Habib – Robaeyat El Khayaam*

2 tablespoons extra-virgin olive oil

2 tablespoons freshly squeezed lemon juice

1 tablespoon freshly squeezed orange juice

1 large clove garlic, minced

1 teaspoon minced, flat-leaf parsley

1 teaspoon minced fresh thyme

1 teaspoon minced fresh chervil

½ teaspoon coarse sea salt

6 zucchini, halved lengthwise

Freshly ground black pepper

THE COMBINATION *of sautéed zucchini and tomatoes that's traditionally eaten during Ramadan in Egypt inspired this dish. It's a lovely side, and you could also eat it as a light meal by topping it with Eggplant, Tomatoes, and Peanuts (page 104), a recipe inspired by the Moroccan dish zaalouk.*

Put the oil, lemon juice, orange juice, garlic, parsley, thyme, chervil, and salt in a large bowl and whisk to combine. Add the zucchini and toss until evenly coated. Cover and refrigerate for at least 3 hours or overnight, tossing occasionally.

Prepare a medium heat grill. Drain the zucchini, arrange on the grill grate, and grill until they begin to char, 4 to 6 minutes. Turn with tongs and cook for 4 to 6 more minutes.

Cut the zucchini into thirds crosswise, transfer to a bowl, sprinkle with pepper, and serve.

PEACH-GLAZED PEARL ONIONS

RAW CANE SUGAR, SEA SALT

YIELD 4 to 6 servings

SOUNDTRACK "Jolin Xica da Silva Komo" by Miriam Makeba from *Country Girl*

Coarse sea salt

1 pound pearl onions

2 ripe peaches, peeled and diced

1 tablespoon raw cane sugar

1 tablespoon water

I WAS INSPIRED TO *create this side dish after reading about the history of onions in ancient Egyptian cooking in The Africa Cookbook, by Jessica B. Harris. Harris explains, "The onion was used in Ancient Egypt to pay tribute to the gods . . . [and onion] remains have even been found in the tomb of King Tutankhamen." Oven roasting softens onions and enhances their natural sweetness. When coated with a sweet puree of peaches, they are lovely and would make a perfect addition to a summer dinner.*

Prepare a large bowl of ice water. Put about 12 cups of water in a large pot and bring to a boil over high heat. Add 1 tablespoon salt, then add the onions and cook for 1 minute. Drain well, immediately plunge the onions into the ice water, and leave until cooled. Drain well. Trim off the roots and slip off the skin from each onion.

Preheat the oven to 425°F. Line a large, rimmed baking sheet with parchment paper.

Put the peaches, sugar, water, and a pinch of salt in a medium saucepan and bring to a simmer over medium heat. Cook, stirring occasionally, until the peaches are soft, about 5 minutes. Transfer to a food processor fitted with the metal blade and process until smooth. Transfer to a large bowl, add the onions and a pinch of salt, and toss until the onions are evenly coated.

Transfer to the lined baking sheet and bake, stirring every 10 minutes, for about 30 minutes, until the onions are soft.

ROASTED PARSNIPS in BARBECUE SAUCE

POMEGRANATE MOLASSES, PEACHES, TOMATO PASTE, CHIPOTLE IN ADOBO SAUCE, OLIVE OIL

YIELD 4 to 6 servings	**SOUNDTRACK** "Everlasting" by Grey Reverend from *A Hero's Lie*	**BOOK** *More Beautiful and More Terrible: TheEmbrace and Transcendence of Racial Inequalityin the United States* by Imani Perry

2 pounds small to medium parsnips, peeled and quartered lengthwise

2 teaspoons extra-virgin olive oil

¼ teaspoon coarse sea salt

½ cup Pomegranate-Peach Barbecue Sauce (page 18)

7 sprigs thyme

THIS RECIPE *is my attempt to help eaters better appreciate the often misunderstood parsnip. Upon first encountering this root vegetable, most people are a bit thrown off: parsnips look like overgrown albino carrots, and their taste is somewhere between a carrot, a rutabaga, and a potato. Inspired by a dish I had at Bartertown Diner, a vegan restaurant in Grand Rapids, Michigan, I roast parsnips to intensify their natural sweetness and then coat them in Pomegranate-Peach Barbecue Sauce.*

Preheat the oven to 450°F. Line a large, rimmed baking sheet with parchment paper.

Put the parsnips in a large bowl, drizzle with the oil, and sprinkle with the salt. Toss until the parsnips are evenly coated.

Transfer to the lined baking sheet (no need to clean the bowl). Bake, stirring every 10 minutes, for about 30 minutes, until fork-tender and beginning to brown. Return the parsnips to the bowl.

Put the barbecue sauce in a small saucepan over medium-high heat and cook, stirring occasionally, until hot. Pour over the parsnips and gently toss until the parsnips are evenly coated. Serve immediately, garnished with the thyme sprigs.

GLAZED CARROT SALAD

CINNAMON, RAW CANE SUGAR, PEANUTS, CILANTRO, MINT

YIELD 6 to 8 servings | **SOUNDTRACK** "Sweet Bite" by George Duke from *The Inner Source*

1¼ pounds carrots (about 10 medium carrots)

1 tablespoon plus ½ teaspoon coarse sea salt

2 tablespoons peanut oil

1 tablespoon freshly squeezed lemon juice

2 teaspoons maple syrup

1 teaspoon ground cinnamon

1 clove garlic, minced

1 teaspoon cumin seeds, toasted (see sidebar, page 9)

¼ cup packed chopped cilantro

2 tablespoons roasted peanuts, crushed

2 tablespoons chopped fresh mint

THIS DISH IS A MASHUP *of glazed carrots, which are popular in the South, and Moroccan carrot salad. The savory coating is rich, intense, and delicious, and as you can see in the photo, this is a gorgeous dish.*

Preheat the oven to 425°F. Line a large roasting pan with parchment paper.

Put about 12 cups of water in a large pot and bring to a boil over high heat. While the water is heating up, cut the carrots into sticks by cutting them in half crosswise, trimming away the edges of each piece to form a rough rectangle, then quartering each rectangle lengthwise. (Compost the scraps or save them for another use.)

When the water is boiling, add 1 tablespoon of the salt, then add the carrots and blanch for 1 minute. Drain the carrots well, then pat them dry with a clean kitchen towel.

Put the oil, lemon juice, maple syrup, cinnamon, garlic, cumin seeds, and the remaining ½ teaspoon salt in a large bowl and mix well. Add the carrots and toss until evenly coated. Transfer to the lined pan (no need to clean the bowl). Cover with aluminum foil and bake for 10 minutes. Remove the foil, gently stir with a wooden spoon, then bake uncovered for about 10 minutes, until the carrots start to brown.

Return the carrots to the bowl. Add the cilantro and toss gently to combine. Serve garnished with the peanuts and mint.

{ continued }

| raw alternative | CARROT SALAD with CARROT-PEANUT DRESSING |

YIELD 4 to 6 servings

CARROT-PEANUT DRESSING

1 medium carrot, coarsely grated (about ½ cup)

⅓ cup skinless raw peanuts

1 pitted Medjool date

½ teaspoon coarse sea salt

⅛ teaspoon ground cinnamon

6 tablespoons water

1 tablespoon freshly squeezed lemon juice

2 teaspoons red wine vinegar

RAW CARROT SALAD

1 pound carrots, shredded

¼ cup packed chopped cilantro

2 tablespoons chopped fresh mint

¼ cup crushed roasted peanuts

This raw carrot salad is for folks looking for some light and refreshing roughage. The dressing is inspired by the peanut sauces served along with yams and plantains in sub-Saharan Africa.

To make the dressing, combine all the ingredients in a blender and process until creamy. Taste and season with more salt if desired.

To make the salad, put the carrots, cilantro, and mint in a medium bowl and toss to combine. Add enough dressing to lightly coat, reserving the rest for another use, and toss well. Serve garnished with the peanuts.

ZA'ATAR-ROASTED RED POTATOES

OLIVE OIL, THYME, OREGANO, LEMON JUICE

YIELD 4 to 6 servings

SOUNDTRACK "The Other Side" by Jihad Muhammad (Bossa Nueva Vocal featuring Malika Zarra) from *The Other Side EP*

2 pounds small to medium red potatoes, cut into ½-inch chunks

3 tablespoons extra-virgin olive oil

2 tablespoons za'atar, homemade (page 15) or store-bought

2 tablespoons minced fresh thyme

1 teaspoon minced fresh oregano

¼ teaspoon fine sea salt

3 tablespoons freshly squeezed lemon juice

Freshly ground black pepper

THIS WAS ONE OF THE *first recipes created for this book. Because I've gotten over-whelmingly positive feedback for my recipe Roasted Red Potato Salad with Parsley–Pine Nut Pesto, published in* Vegan Soul Kitchen, *I wanted to include a dish in this book that could also replace the drowned-in-mayo potato salads that often pop up at summer cookouts. The result: za'atar—a Middle Eastern blend of dried herbs and spices, sesame seeds, and dried sumac—combined with olive oil to make these savory and unctuous potatoes, which would be a fine addition to any table.*

Preheat the oven to 425°F. Line a large, rimmed baking sheet with parchment paper.

Put the potatoes in a large bowl and drizzle with 1 tablespoon of the oil. Toss until the potatoes are evenly coated. Transfer to the lined baking sheet and spread, cut side down, in a single layer (no need to clean the bowl). Bake for 30 minutes.

Meanwhile, combine the za'atar, thyme, oregano, salt, and the remaining 2 tablespoons oil in the reserved bowl and stir well to combine.

Transfer the potatoes to the bowl (leave the oven on) and toss gently until evenly coated. Return the potatoes, cut side up, to the baking sheet and spread in a single layer. Bake for about 15 minutes, until fork-tender.

Transfer to a serving bowl. Sprinkle with the lemon juice and season with black pepper and, if desired, more salt. Serve at room temperature.

SMASHED POTATOES, PEAS, and CORN with CHILE-GARLIC OIL

POTATO, GREEN PEAS, CORN

YIELD 4 to 6 servings

SOUNDTRACK "Ndiri Ndanogio Niwe" by Mbiri Young Stars from *Kenya Special: Selected East African Recordings from the 1970s & '80s*

CHILE-GARLIC OIL
4 teaspoons red pepper flakes

⅓ cup peanut oil

1 large clove garlic, minced

VEGETABLES
3 teaspoons extra-virgin olive oil

2½ teaspoons coarse sea salt

12 small yellow potatoes (about 2 inches in diameter)

2½ cups shelled green peas (about 2½ pounds fresh peas in the pod)

2¼ cups sweet corn kernels (from about 3 ears of corn; store the cobs in the freezer to make Corn Broth, page 43)

¼ cup packed chopped flat-leaf parsley

Freshly ground white pepper

THE TWO MAIN INSPIRATIONS *for the dish are irio and tostones. Irio, the most important cultural dish of the Kikuyu people of Kenya, is a seasoned puree of white potatoes, green peas, and corn, sometimes with spinach or other leafy greens. A hearty staple, it's often served as an accompaniment to stew. Tostones is a popular dish throughout Latin America in which green plantain is sliced crosswise, fried, smashed flat, then fried again to yield a crispy, golden, and scrumptious side dish or snack.*

This recipe is a deconstructed version of irio. Rather than boiling all the ingredients together and mashing, I steam yellow potatoes until tender, smash them like tostones, then bake until crispy. The potatoes are topped with a lightly sautéed mixture of green peas and corn and finished with a drizzle of chile-garlic oil. I like to present this as an all-in-one side dish (starch plus vegetables). It's also a fun appetizer because of the small size of the stacks.

To make the chile oil, put the red pepper flakes in a small heatproof bowl. Warm the peanut oil in a small skillet over medium heat, then add the garlic and sauté until the garlic is fragrant and just starting to turn golden, about 5 minutes. Pour the oil and garlic over the red pepper flakes and let cool, stirring a few times, for about 20 minutes.

To prepare the vegetables, put 2 teaspoons of the olive oil and ¼ teaspoon of the salt in a large bowl and mix.

Put 2 inches of water in a large pot fitted with a steamer insert and bring to a boil. Put the potatoes in the steamer, cover, and cook until fork-tender, adding more water if necessary, about 45 minutes. Remove

the steamer basket from the pot and let the potatoes cool for 5 minutes.

Preheat the oven to 400°F. Line a large, rimmed baking sheet with parchment paper.

Transfer the potatoes to the bowl with the olive oil and toss to coat. On a clean work surface, gently press each potato with the palm of your hand until about ½ inch thick. With a spatula, transfer to the lined baking sheet. Bake for 30 to 35 minutes, until browning and crispy on the edges.

After the potatoes have been baking for 15 minutes, put the remaining 1 teaspoon

{ continued }

olive oil and ¹/₄ teaspoon of the salt in the same bowl and mix well. Put about 8 cups of water in a medium pot and bring to a boil over high heat. Add the remaining 2 teaspoons salt, then add the peas. Return to a boil, and cook uncovered until the peas are just barely tender, 2¹/₂ to 4 minutes. Add the corn and cook for 30 seconds. Drain well, then transfer to the bowl with the olive oil. Add the parsley and toss well.

To serve, top each potato with 3 heaping tablespoons of the pea mixture, drizzle with the chile oil, and finish with a few grinds of white pepper.

NOTE: If you'd like to substitute frozen peas, thaw them, then add to the boiling water along with the corn and cook until just tender, about 5 minutes. To know for certain whether the peas are tender, give one or two a try.

CURRIED SCALLOPED POTATOES
with COCONUT MILK

JAMAICAN CURRY POWDER, HABANERO CHILE, PANKO BREAD CRUMBS, TARRAGON

YIELD 6 to 8 servings

SOUNDTRACK "Good Ways" by Sizzla Kalonji from *Good Ways*

3 tablespoons coconut oil

1 leek, white and tender green parts, thinly sliced (about 1 cup)

1 large clove garlic, minced

¼ to ½ teaspoon minced seeded habanero chile

2 tablespoons Jamaican Curry Powder (page 14)

1¼ teaspoons coarse sea salt

3 cups coconut milk

1¼ cups vegetable stock, homemade (page 42) or store-bought

2¼ pounds Yukon gold potatoes, peeled and sliced into ¼-inch-thick rounds

½ cup panko bread crumbs

2 tablespoons minced fresh tarragon

Freshly ground white pepper

ALTHOUGH FRENCH IN ORIGIN, *scalloped potatoes (or potatoes au gratin) were once fairly common on Southern tables. My mom made the dish regularly, and it was a family favorite. Here, thinly sliced potatoes are simmered in coconut milk laced with Jamaican curry powder, then topped with a mixture of panko bread crumbs, coconut oil, and tarragon, which picks up some of the mustardlike spice in the curry and complements the leek. The potatoes would also make a tasty filling for Jamaican patties (page 122); once they've simmered in the coconut milk, simply dice them and stuff them into the dough, along with some of the coconut milk.*

Warm 1 tablespoon of the oil in a large sauté pan over medium heat. Add the leek and sauté until softened, about 5 minutes. Add the garlic and habanero and sauté until the garlic is fragrant, 2 to 3 minutes. Stir in the curry powder and 1 teaspoon of the salt, then stir in the coconut milk and stock. Stir in the potatoes, increase the heat to medium-high, and bring to a simmer. Immediately decrease the heat to low, cover, and simmer until the potatoes are just fork-tender, about 20 minutes.

Meanwhile, preheat the oven to 400°F and oil a 3-quart baking dish.

With a spoon, gently transfer the potatoes to the oiled baking dish, then pour in all the liquid from the saucepan. Put the bread crumbs, the tarragon, and the remaining 2 tablespoons oil and ¼ teaspoon salt in a small bowl and mix well. Scatter over the potatoes. Bake for 35 to 40 minutes, until the top is golden. Season with white pepper and let cool for 15 minutes before serving.

TWICE-BAKED SWEET POTATOES with WINTER SALSA

PERSIMMON, HAZELNUTS, JALAPEÑO, SCALLIONS, GINGER, CILANTRO

YIELD 4 to 6 servings

SOUNDTRACK "Mi Salsa Buena" by Joe Cuba from *El Pirata del Caribe*

SALSA

2 tablespoons freshly squeezed orange juice

⅛ teaspoon ground cinnamon

¼ teaspoon allspice berries, toasted (see sidebar, page 9) and ground

⅛ teaspoon fine sea salt

4 fuyu persimmons, peeled, seeded, and finely diced

1 jalapeño chile, roasted (see sidebar, page 136), seeded, and diced

1 scallion, white and green parts, thinly sliced

2 tablespoons chopped cilantro

½ teaspoon minced fresh ginger

¼ cup chopped hazelnuts, toasted (see sidebar, page 119)

SWEET POTATOES hold a special place in traditional African-American cookery. For many enslaved Africans, the tuber closely resembled the yams from West Africa, and sweet potatoes became an important staple in African-American cooking. They continue to be emblematic of African-American cuisine, and show up often in the form of candied yams. While persimmons are often associated with Asian cooking, this sweet and delicious fruit has been and continues to be enjoyed in the South (chef Edna Lewis often talked about enjoying them in her youth). While there are many varieties of persimmons, I would imagine that traditionally it was the American persimmon (Diospyros virginiana) that was enjoyed in the South. This variety has to ripen until it is very soft before it can be eaten; otherwise, it is quite astringent, that is, sour and highly tannic. The salsa in this recipe calls for fuyu persimmons (D. kaki), which are ready to eat when they have turned a deep orange but are still firm to the touch. Simple, comforting, and tasty, this recipe can be served as a side dish, yet it's so filling that it can also be offered as an entrée, perhaps with a hearty salad alongside.

To make the salsa, put the orange juice, cinnamon, allspice, and salt in a medium bowl and mix well. Add the persimmons, jalapeño, scallions, cilantro, and ginger and toss well. Let stand at room temperature for at least 1 hour for the flavors to meld. Just before serving, add the hazelnuts and toss gently to combine.

SWEET POTATOES

6 sweet potatoes (about 8 ounces each), scrubbed and patted dry

1 tablespoon coconut oil, plus more for oiling

¼ cup freshly squeezed orange juice

1 teaspoon freshly squeezed lemon juice

1 tablespoons maple syrup

1 teaspoon unsulfured molasses

¼ teaspoon finely grated orange zest

¼ teaspoon finely grated lemon zest

¼ teaspoon grated nutmeg

¼ teaspoon fine sea salt

Meanwhile, prepare the sweet potatoes. Preheat the oven to 425°F. With a fork, pierce the sweet potatoes in about 10 different places, lightly coat with coconut oil, and wrap in aluminum foil. Put them on a baking sheet and bake for 45 to 60 minutes, until fork-tender. Remove from the oven and turn the oven down to 350°F. Let the sweet potatoes cool for about 10 minutes.

Slice off the top one-third (lengthwise) of each sweet potato. Scoop out most of the flesh, leaving a shell about ¼ inch thick, so the sweet potatoes will hold their shape. Transfer the flesh to a bowl. Add the orange juice, lemon juice, oil, maple syrup, molasses, orange zest, lemon zest, nutmeg, and salt and smash with a fork or a potato masher until well combined and mostly smooth.

Fill the sweet potato shells with the mixture, place them on a rimmed baking sheet, and bake for about 10 minutes, until heated through. Serve garnished with the salsa.

GRITS. GRAINS. COUSCOUS.

HISTORICALLY, many of the soup- and stew-centered meals eaten throughout the African continent have been accompanied by a starch to balance flavors and add more heft: there are cornmeal porridges throughout eastern and southern Africa; fermented flatbreads made from teff flour in Ethiopia, Eritria, and other countries in eastern Africa; mashed plantains, cassava, and yams in Central Africa; mashed cassava and cornmeal and rice dishes throughout West Africa; and couscous and flatbreads throughout North Africa.

We also know that many of the starch dishes in the New World have African antecedents. A number of the starchy mashed dishes seen throughout Central and West Africa made their way to the Caribbean and Brazil by way of the transatlantic slave trade and were adapted using local ingredients. Moreover, enslaved Africans from the western part of the continent brought rice to the New World, and it became an important crop in the slave economy of the United States. In fact, the rice economy of the southeastern United States thrived because of the expertise that enslaved Africans brought with them from the rice-growing regions of coastal West Africa. Although corn grits are Native American in origin, this popular African-American dish resembles the porridgelike combination of ground grains and hot water seen throughout the African continent.

This chapter celebrates many of the grains (millet, teff, and rice) and couscous (which is a pasta) seen throughout the African diaspora. A few dishes are hearty enough to be the center of a meal along with a few vegetable sides, and others would make a satisfying accompaniment to a flavorful main. I also offer a flavorful salad made from wheat berries in honor of a friend who got me hooked on them. In the end, I want this chapter to serve as a model for ways to creatively mix grits, grains, or couscous with farm-fresh vegetables to produce flavorful and satisfying combinations. I hope that all of these recipes help elevate grains from afterthoughts to exciting features in your daily meals.

CINNAMON-SOAKED WHEAT BERRY SALAD

DRIED APRICOTS, CARROT, ALMONDS, CILANTRO

YIELD 4 to 6 servings | **SOUNDTRACK** "Galou" by Nass Marrakech from *Bouderbala*

SALAD

- 1 cup wheat berries
- 3 cups boiling water
- 1 (2-inch) cinnamon stick
- 1¼ teaspoons coarse sea salt
- 3 carrots (about 8 ounces total), diced into ¼-inch pieces
- 1 heaping cup thinly sliced dried apricots
- 6 tablespoons packed minced cilantro
- ½ cup almonds, blanched (see sidebar, page 152), toasted (see sidebar, page 119), and chopped

DRESSING

- 3 tablespoons apple cider vinegar
- 1 tablespoon freshly squeezed lemon juice
- 1 heaping teaspoon Dijon mustard
- 1 teaspoon maple syrup
- ½ teaspoon fine sea salt
- ¼ teaspoon ground cinnamon
- 3 tablespoons extra-virgin olive oil

Freshly ground white pepper

THIS SALAD, INSPIRED BY *autumn earth tones (orange, green, rust, and brown) and flavors typical of some Moroccan tagines, is dedicated to my friend Heidi Swanson, blogger, entrepreneur, and cookbook author. Heidi has probably done more than anyone to make wheat berries sexy and appealing. She sure got me excited about them. Beyond that, she's played such an important role in the growth of my career, and her work continues to inspire me to step up my game. Check out her website (101cookbooks.com) and try some of her recipes.*

To make the salad, put the wheat berries in a medium saucepan. Pour in the boiling water, cover, and let cool to room temperature. Refrigerate for at least 8 hours or overnight.

Add the cinnamon stick and ¼ teaspoon of the salt and bring to a boil over high heat. Decrease the heat to low, cover, and simmer until tender but chewy, about 1 hour. Remove from the heat and let sit with the lid on for 15 minutes. Drain if necessary and remove the cinnamon stick.

Meanwhile, prepare a medium bowl of ice water. Put about 4 cups of water in a medium saucepan and bring to a boil over high heat. Add the remaining 1 teaspoon salt, then add the carrots and cook uncovered until fork-tender, about 2 minutes. Drain well, then immediately plunge the carrots into the ice water to stop the cooking. Drain well. Transfer to a large bowl. Add the wheat berries, apricots, cilantro, and almonds and mix well.

To make the dressing, combine the vinegar, lemon juice, mustard, maple syrup, salt, and cinnamon in a blender. With the blender running, slowly pour in the oil and process until creamy.

To serve, pour the dressing over the salad and toss well with clean hands. Cover and refrigerate for 1 hour to allow flavors to meld. Remove from the refrigerator about 30 minutes before serving to bring to room temperature. Season with white pepper to taste just before serving.

COUSCOUS with BUTTERNUT SQUASH, PECANS, and CURRANTS

SAFFRON, DATES, CINNAMON

YIELD 4 to 6 servings | **SOUNDTRACK** "Persian Love Song" by Dead Can Dance from *Toward the Within*

3 tablespoons extra-virgin olive oil, plus more for oiling

1 pound butternut squash, peeled and cut into ½-inch pieces

1 teaspoon coarse sea salt

1⅓ cups whole wheat couscous

1½ cups water

Large pinch of saffron threads

¾ cup currants

2 Medjool dates, pitted

½ cup chopped pecans

½ teaspoon ground cinnamon

2 tablespoons packed torn fresh mint leaves

Freshly ground white pepper

THIS TASTY, SWEET-LEANING *side dish would be an excellent accompaniment to a savory stew.*

Preheat the oven to 425°F. Line a large, rimmed baking sheet with parchment paper. Oil a 2-quart baking dish

Put the butternut squash in a large bowl. Drizzle with 1 tablespoon of the oil, sprinkle with ¼ teaspoon of the salt, and toss until the squash is evenly coated. Transfer to the lined baking sheet and bake, stirring after 15 minutes, for 30 to 40 minutes, until the squash is soft and just starting to brown on the edges. Remove from the oven and turn the oven down to 350°F.

Meanwhile, warm 1 tablespoon of the oil in a medium saucepan over medium-high heat. Add the couscous and toast, stirring often, just until it starts to smell fragrant, 2 to 3 minutes. Remove from the heat.

Put the water and the remaining ¾ teaspoon salt in a small saucepan and bring to a boil. Remove from the heat, add the saffron, and let sit for 1 minute. Pour over the couscous, add the currants, and stir well. Cover and let sit for 10 minutes.

Put the dates in a small bowl and add boiling water to cover. Let soak for about 5 minutes. Drain, reserving the liquid, and put the dates and 2 tablespoons of the soaking liquid in a blender. Add the remaining 2 tablespoons oil and process until creamy.

Transfer to a medium skillet over medium-high heat. Add the pecans and cook, stirring constantly, until thoroughly combined, about 3 minutes. Scrape the contents of the skillet into the couscous and toss to combine, breaking up any big lumps of couscous. Transfer to the oiled baking dish, cover with aluminum foil, and bake for 15 minutes, until heated through.

To serve, pile the couscous in a high mound on a large serving platter. Make an indentation in the top and spoon in some of the butternut squash. Scatter the remaining squash around the edges. Sprinkle the cinnamon over the mound in even vertical stripes. Garnish with the mint, and give a few turns of white pepper.

CRISPY TEFF and GRIT CAKES with EGGPLANT, TOMATOES, and PEANUTS

TEFF, GRITS, EGGPLANT, TOMATO, ROASTED GARLIC

YIELD 4 to 8 servings || **SOUNDTRACK** "Ethio Blues" by Mulatu Astatke from *Mulatu Steps Ahead*

GRITS

4 cups vegetable stock, homemade (page 42) or store-bought

1 tablespoon extra-virgin olive oil

½ teaspoon coarse sea salt

¾ cup yellow grits

¼ cup teff

½ cup Creamed Cashews (page 143)

EGGPLANT AND TOMATOES

1½ pounds globe eggplant, peeled and cut into ½-inch pieces

1 tablespoon plus ¼ teaspoon coarse sea salt

½ cup finely diced red onion

¾ teaspoon cumin seeds, toasted (see sidebar, page 9) and ground

½ teaspoon coriander seeds, toasted (see sidebar, page 9) and ground

2 teaspoons paprika

¼ teaspoon red pepper flakes

Pinch of cayenne pepper

2 tablespoons extra-virgin olive oil, plus more for frying

1 small head garlic, roasted (see sidebar, page 106)

2 pounds heirloom tomatoes, peeled, seeded, and finely diced (see sidebar, page 106)

¾ cup water

½ teaspoon freshly squeezed lemon juice

½ cup unsalted roasted peanuts

¼ cup packed chopped flat-leaf parsley

CREAMY, CRUNCHY, SAVORY, TANGY—*this dish hits all the right notes. In the traditional Southern kitchens of working and poor people, folks made use of every bit of food available, and the perfect way to transform stiff leftover grits into a tasty dish was to slice them, panfry them, and eat them with something sweet and syrupy.*

This dish, an East African–Deep South hybrid, combines the Ethiopian grain teff with stone-ground corn grits. The crispy panfried cakes work equally well as a sweet breakfast item or a savory entrée for lunch or dinner. The savory sauce is my version of zaalouk, a Moroccan dish made with eggplant, tomatoes, garlic, and spices. In North Africa, zaalouk is eaten as a dip with bread, presented as part of an array of salads, or served as an accompaniment to main dishes like tagines or fish. Here, the intense, tangy sauce serves as a perfect foil for simple, crispy cakes.

To make the grits, put the stock, oil, and salt in a medium saucepan and bring to a boil over medium-high heat. Slowly pour in the grits and teff, whisking constantly until no lumps remain. Return to a boil, stir in the Creamed Cashews, then immediately decrease the heat to low and simmer uncovered for 25 minutes, stirring every 2 to 3 minutes with a wooden spoon to prevent sticking.

Lightly oil a 7 by 11-inch baking dish. Scrape the grits into the dish and spread evenly with a rubber spatula. Cover and refrigerate until firm, at least 3 hours or overnight.

About 1 hour before serving, prepare the eggplant and tomatoes. Combine the eggplant and 1 tablespoon of the salt in a large bowl and toss well. Set aside for 30 minutes. Preheat an oven to 400°F and line a baking sheet with parchment paper.

Rinse the eggplant in a colander with cold water, then squeeze with a clean kitchen towel to dry. Transfer the eggplant to the

{ continued }

prepared baking sheet and roast, stirring after 15 minutes, for about 30 minutes, until browning.

Next, combine the onion, cumin, coriander, paprika, red pepper flakes, cayenne, and the remaining 1/4 teaspoon salt with the oil in a large sauté pan over medium-low heat. Sauté, stirring often with a wooden spoon, until the onion is soft, 5 to 7 minutes. Add all the roasted garlic cloves, mash them with the back of the wooden spoon, and stir well to combine. Increase the heat to high, then add the tomatoes, water, and the reserved eggplant. Stir well to combine, cover, lower the heat to medium, and simmer, stirring occasionally, until the mixture starts to thicken, about 25 minutes. Stir in the lemon juice.

To serve, preheat the oven to 250°F. Turn the grits out onto a clean work surface, keeping them in one piece. Trim away 1/2 inch from all four sides. (Compost the trimmings or fry the pieces and eat for breakfast.) Cut the grits into 8 even rectangles. Line a couple large plates with paper towels.

Warm about 1 tablespoon oil in a large nonstick skillet over medium-high heat. When the oil is hot but not smoking, add as many teff cakes as can fit without crowding. Panfry until deeply brown and crispy on the outside, 3 to 4 minutes per side. Transfer the cooked cakes to the lined plates to drain and hold them in the oven until all the cakes are cooked.

Serve each cake topped with a heaping 1/3 cup (or more) of the eggplant mixture and garnished with the peanuts and parsley.

ROASTING GARLIC

To roast garlic, preheat the oven to 350°F. Cut 1/4 inch off the top of 1 large head garlic to expose its cloves. Put the garlic head, cut side up, on a piece of aluminum foil, pour 3 tablespoons extra-virgin olive oil over the garlic, and wrap the head in the foil. Place on a baking sheet or in a small pan to prevent the oil from dripping into the oven and bake for about 1 hour, until the garlic is caramelizing and tender. Remove from the oven and let cool.

PEELING TOMATOES

To peel a tomato, cut out the stem, then slice a shallow X on the bottom. Prepare a bowl of ice water and bring a pot of water to a boil. With a slotted spoon, lower the tomato into the hot water for 5 seconds, then plunge it into the ice water. Peel away the skin.

CURRIED CORN and COCONUT RICE

SWEET CORN, CURRY POWDER, SHORT-GRAIN BROWN RICE, COCONUT MILK, DRIED COCONUT

YIELD 4 to 6 servings	SOUNDTRACK "Bokul Phool" by Joler Gaan from *Otol Joler Gaan*	BOOK *Bright Lines* by Tanwi Nandini Islam

RICE

¾ cup coconut milk

1½ cups water

½ teaspoon coarse sea salt

1 cup short-grain brown rice, soaked in water overnight and drained well

2 tablespoons unsweetened shredded dried coconut

CORN

1¼ teaspoons coarse sea salt

Kernels from 5 ears of sweet corn (store the cobs in the freezer to make Corn Broth, page 43)

1 tablespoon extra-virgin olive oil

1 clove garlic, minced

½ teaspoon Jamaican Curry Powder (page 14)

THE COCONUT RICE *and curried corn in this recipe could very well be eaten separately, and they would make fine additions to lunch or dinner, but the combination of the two is truly special. I call for Jamaican Curry Powder, giving the corn a complexly spicy, sweet, and slightly sour flavor profile.*

To prepare the rice, combine the coconut milk, water, and salt in a medium saucepan and bring to a boil over high heat. Add the rice and dried coconut, stir well, and return to a boil. Immediately decrease the heat to low, cover, and simmer until all of the liquid is absorbed and the rice is tender, about 50 minutes. Remove from the heat and let sit, covered, for at least 10 minutes. Fluff with a fork before serving.

To prepare the corn, put about 8 cups of water in a medium pot and bring to a boil over high heat. Add 1 teaspoon of the salt, then add the corn. Immediately remove from the heat and let sit for 30 seconds. Drain well.

Warm the oil in a medium sauté pan over medium heat. Add the garlic, curry powder, and the remaing ¼ teaspoon salt and sauté until fragrant, about 2 minutes. Add the corn and sauté until heated through, 3 to 5 minutes.

To serve, spoon the corn over the rice.

SAVORY GRITS with SLOW-COOKED COLLARD GREENS

COLLARD GREENS, GINGER, JALAPEÑO, RED BELL PEPPER

YIELD 4 to 6 servings   ‖   **SOUNDTRACK** "The Funk" by Oh No from *Dr. No's Ethiopium*

GREENS

- 1 tablespoon plus ¼ teaspoon coarse sea salt
- 1 pound collard greens, cut into bite-size pieces
- 3 tablespoons extra-virgin olive oil
- 1 red onion, finely chopped
- ½ teaspoon minced fresh ginger
- ¼ teaspoon chili powder
- ⅛ teaspoon cayenne pepper
- 2 large cloves garlic, minced
- 1 cup vegetable stock, homemade (page 42) or store-bought
- 1 large red bell pepper, diced
- 1 jalapeño chile, seeded and minced

(continued on page 110)

"GRITS AND GREENS," a regular series of breakfast gatherings put together by my friend Ashara Ekundayo and Hub Oakland, explores the intersection of food, art, and technology. The events bring together "innovators, educators, artists, makers, hackers, and entrepreneurs living and working in the cross sections of these fields." I had the pleasure of sitting on a panel at the inaugural convening held at Miss Ollie's, a Caribbean restaurant in Oakland, California, along with Majora Carter (Startup Box: South Bronx) and Edward West (hylo.com).

Each gathering features creamy grits (always including a vegan option) along with a variety of sweet and savory finishes, such as Brazilian-style collard greens, crispy Southern-style eggplant with silken tofu, brown sugar–coated roasted bananas, sautéed mixed field greens, and grilled tofu. As a shout-out to Ashara and the Hub Oakland crew I offer these creamy grits topped with my version of Ethiopian greens (gomen wat). Of course you can also experiment with different savory toppings for your grits or try the greens as a side with other dishes.

To make the greens, put about 12 cups of water in a large pot and bring to a boil over high heat. Add 1 tablespoon of the salt, then add the greens and cook uncovered until softened, about 10 minutes. Drain well, pressing the greens to extract as much liquid as possible. When cool enough to handle, transfer to a cutting board and chop finely.

Warm the oil in a medium sauté pan over medium heat. Add the onion, ginger, chili powder, cayenne, and the remaining ¼ teaspoon salt. Sauté until the onion is soft and beginning to brown, about 10 minutes. Add the garlic and sauté for 2 minutes. Stir in the greens and stock and bring to a simmer. Decrease the heat to medium-low, cover, and simmer, stirring occasionally, until the greens are tender, about 45 minutes. Stir in the bell pepper and jalapeño. Increase the heat to medium-high, cover, and simmer for 2 minutes. Taste and season with more salt if desired.

{ continued }

GRITS

4 cups vegetable stock, homemade (page 42) or store-bought

1 teaspoon coarse sea salt

¾ cup yellow corn grits

½ cup Creamed Cashews (page 143)

¼ cup packed minced flat-leaf parsley

Hot-pepper vinegar, homemade (page 20) or store-bought, for serving

Freshly ground black pepper

While the greens are simmering, make the grits. Put 3 cups of the stock and the salt in a medium saucepan and bring to a boil over high heat. Slowly pour in the grits, whisking constantly until no lumps remain. Return to a boil, then immediately decrease the heat to low. Simmer uncovered, whisking occasionally to prevent sticking, until the grits have absorbed most of the liquid and are beginning to thicken, 3 to 5 minutes. Add the remaining 1 cup stock and simmer for 10 minutes, whisking occasionally, until most of the liquid has been absorbed. Stir in the cashew cream, cover, and simmer, whisking frequently, until the grits are soft and fluffy, about 30 minutes.

Add the parsley and whisk well. The grits should be firm and creamy. Add a bit of water to thin them if necessary.

To serve, top the grits with the greens, using a slotted spoon so that the liquid drains from the greens. Add a splash of hot-pepper vinegar and season with black pepper.

DIRTY MILLET

TEMPEH, PORCINI, CREMINI, AND SHIITAKE MUSHROOMS

YIELD 4 to 6 servings | **SOUNDTRACK** "Dougou Badia" by Amadou and Mariam (featuring Santigold) from *Folila*

½ cup sliced dried porcini mushrooms

2 cups boiling water

2 tablespoons plus 1 teaspoon extra-virgin olive oil, plus more for drizzling

½ cup finely diced yellow onion

½ cup finely diced green bell pepper

½ cup diced celery, strings removed (see sidebar, page 74)

⅛ teaspoon cayenne pepper

¾ teaspoon coarse sea salt

6 ounces tempeh, crumbled

1 tablespoon tamari

4 ounces cremini mushrooms, stemmed and thinly sliced

4 ounces shiitake mushrooms, stemmed and thinly sliced

1 cup millet, soaked in water overnight and drained well

1 cup vegetable stock, homemade (page 42) or store-bought

Freshly ground black pepper

2 tablespoons minced flat-leaf parsley

I IMAGINE THAT DIRTY RICE, *a traditional Cajun rice pilaf, was created as a way to ensure that no parts of a bird went to waste and to add flavor to plain rice. Here I have reinvented dirty rice, replacing the white rice with millet and the giblets with a mixture of tempeh and porcini, cremini, and shiitake mushrooms. The tempeh and mushroom mixture adds depth, making this a filling main dish.*

Put the porcini in a small heatproof bowl and pour in the boiling water, making sure it covers them (you may need to weight the mushrooms with another small bowl). Let soak for 20 minutes. Drain through a fine-mesh sieve, reserving the soaking liquid, and chop the porcini finely.

Warm 1 tablespoon of the oil in a medium sauté pan over medium heat. Add the onion, bell pepper, celery, cayenne, and ¼ teaspoon of the salt and sauté until the vegetables begin to soften, about 5 minutes. Add another tablespoon of the oil and the tempeh, increase the heat to medium-high, and cook, stirring occasionally, until the tempeh begins to brown and crisp, about 5 minutes. Drizzle in the tamari and add the cremini, shiitakes, porcini, and ¼ teaspoon of the salt. Decrease the heat to medium and sauté until the mushrooms release their liquid and begin to brown, about 5 minutes. Transfer to a bowl.

In the same sauté pan, toast the millet over medium heat, stirring often, until the millet starts to smell nutty, about 3 minutes. Transfer to a medium saucepan. Stir in the stock, 1 cup of the reserved porcini mushroom liquid, and the remaining ¼ teaspoon salt, 1 teaspoon oil, and the tempeh mixture. Bring to a boil over high heat. Immediately decrease the heat to low, cover, and simmer, until all the liquid is absorbed, about 15 minutes. Turn off the heat and let sit, covered, for 15 minutes.

Season to taste with black pepper and, if desired, more salt. Serve garnished with the parsley and drizzled with olive oil.

VERDANT VEGETABLE COUSCOUS with SPICY MUSTARD GREENS

ASPARAGUS, BROCCOLINI, FRESH HERBS, LEMON

YIELD 4 to 6 servings ‖ **SOUNDTRACK** "Couscous" by Richard Bona from *Munia (The Tale)*

2 tablespoons plus 2 teaspoons extra-virgin olive oil

1⅓ cups whole wheat couscous

1¾ cups vegetable stock, homemade (page 42) or store-bought

3 tablespoons Spicy Mustard Greens (page 25), plus more for serving

1 tablespoon plus ¾ teaspoon coarse sea salt

1 pound thin asparagus, ends trimmed, tips removed, and stalks cut into ¼-inch-thick slices

8 ounces broccolini, sliced ¼ inch thick

1 tablespoon freshly squeezed lemon juice

1 tablespoon minced fresh chives

1 tablespoon minced flat-leaf parsley

I CREATED THIS RECIPE to *showcase asparagus, broccolini, and spring herbs. The Spicy Mustard Greens gives the couscous a grassy-peppery essence, and the vegetables and fresh herbs piled on top are mouthwatering. You can serve this dish alone as a hearty salad or pair it with a soup, stew, or tagine. If broccolini is not available, you can use broccoli.*

Put about 8 cups of water in a medium pot and bring to a boil over high heat. While the water heats up, warm 1 tablespoon of the oil in a medium skillet over medium-high heat. Add the couscous and toast, stirring often, just until it starts to smell fragrant, 3 to 4 minutes. Remove from the heat.

Put the stock, Spicy Mustard Greens, and ¼ teaspoon of the salt in a small saucepan and bring to a boil over high heat, whisking until the salt dissolves. Pour over the couscous and stir well. Cover and let stand for 5 minutes.

When the water is boiling, add 1 tablespoon of the salt, then add the asparagus tips and sliced stalks and the broccolini. Immediately remove from the heat and let sit for 2 minutes. Drain well, then transfer to a bowl. Drizzle with 2 teaspoons of the oil, sprinkle with ½ teaspoon of the salt, and toss gently until evenly coated.

Fluff the couscous with a fork. Drizzle with the lemon juice and the remaining 1 tablespoon oil and toss until evenly coated. Transfer to a serving dish and top with the asparagus, broccolini, and fresh herbs. Serve additional Spicy Mustard Greens alongside.

NOTE: For a gluten-free version, substitute 1⅓ cups quinoa for the couscous and increase the vegetable stock to 2½ cups. Follow the recipe as directed. When the stock and Spicy Mustard Greens are boiling, add the quinoa and simmer over low heat until all the liquid has been absorbed, about 15 minutes. Let sit for 5 minutes before topping with the vegetables.

STREET FOOD. SNACKS. SMALL BITES.

GROWING UP, one of my favorite snacks was the handmade tamales sold by old black men on Third Street near the Crystal Palace Roller Skating Rink in Memphis, Tennessee. When I was living in Brooklyn, I ate Jamaican veggie patties sold at small take-out windows in Crown Heights and Bed-Stuy several times per week. And when I travel internationally, I find that vendors hawking their culinary creations on the street tend to have the best-tasting (and least expensive) ready-to-eat food. These personal memories were a major inspiration for this chapter, and I am excited about the growing number of restaurant-quality food carts and food trucks popping up in cities across the United States.

I also think it is important to look back and recognize the history of global street food that predates many of the ready-to-eat snacks and on-the-go meals that we are familiar with today. Historically, selling street food has provided many poor people with a means of generating income outside of the formal economy, and poor and working-poor people have been the primary consumers of cheap, filling, and portable food. In contrast, many of the emerging street-food cultures in major cities across the United States have moved beyond cheap eats for everyday people and are now serving gourmet foods with higher prices that would be a splurge for the average Joe. I created the recipes in this chapter in honor of regular working people.

Here are my takes on fun (a number of them are fried), casual foods that you might find in major cities and rural areas throughout Africa, the Caribbean, and the United States, such as Sweet Plantain and Fresh Corn Cakes (page 129) that would be at home at a chop bar in Accra, Ghana; Jamaican Patties Stuffed with Maque Choux (page 122) that could be found at a take-out shop in Port Antonio, Jamaica; and Lemongrass Boiled Peanuts (page 121), a twist on what you might see at a roadside farm stand in Collins, Mississippi. Of course, most of these dishes can serve multiple functions: they're quick snacks to tide you over, finger foods to be enjoyed with drinks, and appetizers to warm you up for a larger meal. It's up to you.

CHERMOULA TEMPEH BITES

OLIVE OIL, VEGETABLE STOCK

YIELD 8 to 12 servings as an hors d'oeuvre, or 4 to 6 servings as a main dish

SOUNDTRACK "An Echo from the Hosts That Profess Infinitum" by Shabazz Palaces from *Black Up*

6 tablespoons extra-virgin olive oil

1 pound tempeh, cut into ½-inch cubes

2 cups vegetable stock, homemade (page 42) or store-bought

1½ cups Chermoula (page 16)

½ teaspoon coarse sea salt

CHERMOULA, *an herb-filled sauce used in North African cooking, is a delicious marinade in which to bake tempeh. These tasty morsels can be eaten alone as an hors d'oeuvre, or serve them as a main dish, along with couscous or rice.*

Preheat the oven to 350°F.

Warm 1 tablespoon of the oil in a large nonstick skillet over medium-high heat until very hot but not smoking. Add the tempeh in a single layer and cook, tilting the pan to spread the oil evenly among the tempeh cubes, until golden on the bottom, 3 to 5 minutes. With a fork, turn the tempeh on the opposite side. Add another tablespoon of the oil and cook until the cubes are golden on the bottom, 3 to 5 minutes. Repeat this process until all 6 sides are golden. Transfer to a large bowl.

Put the stock, Chermoula, and salt in a medium saucepan and bring to a boil over high heat. Immediately pour three-fourths of the mixture over the tempeh, reserving the remainder. Stir gently until the tempeh is evenly coated, then immediately transfer to a 2-quart baking dish, spreading the tempeh in a single snug layer. Cover tightly with aluminum foil and bake for 1 hour, until much of the sauce has been absorbed.

Remove the foil, add the remaining Chermoula mixture, and stir gently until evenly incorporated. Bake for 10 minutes, until warmed though. Serve at room temperature.

SUGARED PECANS

SUNFLOWER OIL, RAW CANE SUGAR

YIELD
4 cups

SOUNDTRACK "Stuck Together Pieces" by Atoms for Peace from *Amok*

4 cups pecan halves, toasted (see sidebar)

3 tablespoons sunflower oil

¼ cup raw cane sugar

SIMPLE AND SWEET, *these nuts can be enjoyed as a snack or as a sugary bite after a meal. I also use them to add texture to other desserts. I really like pecans prepared this way, but I encourage you to experiment with other nuts to see what moves you.*

Put the pecans in a large bowl. Drizzle with the oil and stir until thoroughly coated. Sprinkle with the sugar and stir until thoroughly coated. Warm a large, dry cast-iron skillet over medium-high heat until hot. Add the pecans, scraping the bowl to get everything into the skillet, and cook, stirring constantly, until the pecans are fragrant and most of the liquid has evaporated, about 1½ minutes. Transfer the pecans to a sheet of parchment paper and quickly spread them out, separating them with 2 forks. Let cool to room temperature. Stored in a sealed container at room temperature, the pecans will keep for a few weeks.

TOASTING NUTS AND SEEDS

Toasted nuts and seeds add texture, unique flavors, and protein to salads, stir-fries, and other dishes. To bring out their natural oil and enhance their taste, toast them in a dry skillet over medium heat, shaking often, until fragrant, about 4 minutes; or toast on a baking sheet in an oven at 325°F for 5 to 7 minutes, shaking the pan a few times for even cooking. Nuts and seeds contain oils that will go rancid, so store them in a freezer.

MOLASSES-GLAZED WALNUTS

SUNFLOWER OIL, RAW CANE SUGAR, SALT

YIELD
2 cups

SOUNDTRACK "Givin Em What They Love" by Janelle Monáe (featuring Prince) from *The Electric Lady*

2 cups walnut pieces

1 tablespoon sunflower oil

2 tablespoons unsulfured molasses

1 tablespoon raw cane sugar

¼ teaspoon fine sea salt

I CREATED THESE FOR *Sweet Potato Granola (page 165), but they are heavenly by themselves.*

Preheat the oven to 350°F. Line a large, rimmed baking sheet with parchment paper.

Spread the walnuts on the lined baking sheet and bake, stirring after 4 minutes, for 8 minutes, until fragrant and starting to toast. Set aside until cool enough to handle. Transfer to a sieve and, holding the sieve over the sink, rub the walnuts against the wire until their skins loosen and fall off.

Put the walnuts in a large bowl. Drizzle with the oil and stir until evenly coated. Drizzle with the molasses and stir until evenly coated, then sprinkle with the sugar and salt and stir until evenly coated.

Warm a large, dry cast-iron skillet over medium-high heat. Add the walnuts, scraping the bowl to get all of the seasonings into the skillet. Cook, stirring constantly, until the walnuts are fragrant, about 3 minutes. Transfer the walnuts to a sheet of parchment paper and quickly spread them out, separating them with two forks. Let cool to room temperature. Stored in a sealed container at room temperature, the walnuts will keep for a few weeks.

LEMONGRASS BOILED PEANUTS

LEMONGRASS, SEA SALT

YIELD	SOUNDTRACK "Feather" by Little Dragon from *Machine Dreams*
1 cup	

1 pound raw green or dried peanuts in the shell

6 cups water

3 tablespoons coarse sea salt

2 lemongrass stalks, ends trimmed and thinly sliced

BOILED PEANUTS *are made by boiling raw "green" peanuts for a long time. Green peanuts are freshly harvested and have a higher moisture content. They are generally available from online retailers from May through November, and sometimes you can find them at Asian markets or farmers' markets in the South during that period. Raw peanuts that have been dried can also be used for boiled peanuts, and they are generally easier to find than green ones. If using raw green peanuts, boil them for about 3 hours; dried peanuts will need 6 hours or longer. Note: Roasted peanuts should not be used for this recipe.*

Put the peanuts in a colander and rinse them thoroughly. Transfer to a stockpot and add the water, salt, and lemongrass. Bring to a boil over high heat. Decrease the heat to medium-low, cover, and simmer until soft, about 3 hours if using green peanuts or 6 hours if using dried peanuts. Remove from the heat and let soak for 2 hours. Drain well. Store in a refrigerator and eat within 3 days.

JAMAICAN PATTIES STUFFED
with MAQUE CHOUX

SWEET CORN, TOMATO, GREEN BELL PEPPER

YIELD	SOUNDTRACK "Brass in Africa" by Hypnotic Brass	FILM: *Life and Debt* directed by
6 servings	Ensemble from *Best of BBE 2011*	Stephanie Black

PASTRY

3 cups unbleached all-purpose flour, chilled

2 cups whole wheat pastry flour, chilled

1 tablespoon ground turmeric

¾ teaspoon fine sea salt

2 cups coconut oil, chilled

4 teaspoons apple cider vinegar

1 tablespoon plus ¾ teaspoon ice water

BACK IN 2009, *Emeril Lagasse invited me to be a guest on his television show Emeril Green. I drove up to Napa Valley to film inside the Culinary Institute of America at Greystone and spent the whole day cooking with him for an episode entitled "Vegan Soul Cookin'." We made a few recipes from Vegan Soul Kitchen, along with some classic Cajun and Creole dishes—veganized, of course. One of my favorite recipes that day was maque choux—a traditional dish of southern Louisiana made of corn, tomatoes, bell pepper, and onion (and often bacon grease, butter, or cream).*

Although it's usually served as a side dish, I thought maque choux would make a tasty filling for a Jamaican patty, a baked pastry eaten as a snack in Jamaica and other Caribbean countries. Serve these as appetizers at a party along with Chipotle-Banana Pepper Sauce (page 19). They also work well as an entrée if served with a side dish or two. In the unlikely event that you have leftover patties, you can freeze them for a quick snack at a later time.

To make the pastry, put the flours, turmeric, and salt in a large bowl and mix well. Add the coconut oil and rub with your fingertips until the mixture resembles fine sand; this could take as long as 10 minutes.

Stir the vinegar and water together. Then, without overworking the dough, add the vinegar mixture, 1 tablespoon at a time while stirring. As soon as the dough comes away from the sides of the bowl and holds together, squeeze it into a tight ball. Flatten into a disk, wrap in plastic wrap, and refrigerate until chilled, at least 1 hour.

FILLING

2 teaspoons coconut oil

1/2 cup finely diced red onion

1/4 cup finely diced green bell pepper

1/2 teaspoon minced seeded habanero chile

1 teaspoon coarse sea salt

1/2 teaspoon cumin seeds, toasted (see sidebar, page 9) and ground

1/2 teaspoon allspice berries, toasted (see sidebar, page 9) and ground

1/8 teaspoon ground cinnamon

1/8 teaspoon cayenne pepper

1 1/4 cups sweet corn kernels (from about 2 ears of corn; store the cobs in the freezer to make Corn Broth, page 43)

1/2 cup peeled (see sidebar, page 106), seeded, and finely diced firm heirloom tomato

3/4 cup coconut milk

1/2 teaspoon freshly squeezed lime juice

1 tablespoon minced fresh thyme

Freshly ground black pepper

Meanwhile, make the filling. Warm the oil in a medium sauté pan over medium heat. Add the onion, bell pepper, habanero, salt, cumin, allspice, cinnamon, and cayenne and sauté until the onion and bell pepper are very soft, 10 to 12 minutes. Stir in the corn, tomato, and coconut milk. Decrease the heat to low. partially cover, and cook, stirring occasionally, until the corn is tender, 8 to 10 minutes. Stir in the lime juice and thyme and cook until warmed through, 2 to 3 minutes. Season with black pepper and, if desired, more salt.

To assemble and bake the patties, remove the dough from the refrigerator to warm slightly. Preheat the oven to 350°F. Line a baking sheet with parchment paper.

After the dough has warmed for about 20 minutes, lightly flour a work surface. Roll out the dough about 1/8 inch thick. Cut six 6-inch circles from the dough. Spoon a little less than 3 heaping tablespoons of the filling onto each circle, placing it on one side and leaving about a 1/8-inch border. Fold the other side over to make a half-moon. Press to seal, then use the tines of a fork to make ridges around the sealed edge. (Enjoy any leftover filling as a side dish.)

Transfer the patties to the lined baking sheet and bake for about 40 minutes, until golden brown. Serve immediately.

CREOLE-SPICED PLANTAIN CHIPS

GREEN PLANTAIN, PAPRIKA, CHILI POWDER, RED PEPPER FLAKES, CAYENNE

YIELD
4 servings

SOUNDTRACK "Dr. Carter" by Lil Wayne from *Tha Carter III*

4 large green plantains (about 2 pounds)

¼ cup Creole spice blend, homemade (page 12) or store-bought

Coconut or sunflower oil, for deep-frying (about 5 cups)

KELEWELE, *a classic Ghanaian snack of fried plantains that have been seasoned with spices, was the initial inspiration for this dish. But instead of cutting the plantains into chunks, I slice them as thinly as possible, more in the style of plantain chips, popular in other countries throughout West Africa and in the Caribbean. Coating the chips in a Creole spice mixture adds intense flavor and a little heat. Make sure you use green plantains, as ripe, yellow plantains won't develop the crispy texture that makes this such a satisfying snack.*

Cut off both ends of each plantain. With the tip of a sharp knife, slice the peel along the length of each plantain, avoiding cutting into the flesh. Repeat this in three different places on each plantain. Gently remove each section of peel. (Compost the peels and tips.) If the peels are difficult to remove, soak the plantains in hot water for a few minutes. Just be sure to dry them well with a clean kitchen towel before frying, to prevent splattering. With a sharp knife or a mandoline, slice each plantain as thinly as possible into rounds, ideally about 1/16 inch thick, keeping the slices of each plantain separate.

Put 1 tablespoon of the spice blend in a small paper bag. Line a plate with paper towels.

Warm about 2 inches of oil in a large, heavy pot over medium-high heat until hot but not smoking, about 375°F. Fry the slices of 1 plantain at a time, moving them around with a fork to ensure even cooking, until golden, about 1 minute. With a skimmer or slotted spoon, immediately transfer the slices to the paper bag with the spice mixture. Fold the top to seal, then shake vigorously to evenly coat. Transfer to the lined plate. Repeat this process with the remaining plantains and spice blend. Serve while they are hot and crispy.

LIL' TOFU PO'BOYS with CREAMY RED BELL PEPPER SAUCE

PANKO BREAD CRUMBS, CREOLE SPICE BLEND

YIELD 4 lil' sandwiches

SOUNDTRACK "Long John Blues" by Renee Wilson from *Voodoo Queen*

2 (1-pound) blocks extra-firm tofu

1 cup water

¼ cup tamari

2 tablespoons freshly squeezed orange juice

1 tablespoon apple cider vinegar

1 teaspoon freshly squeezed lemon juice

1 large clove garlic, minced

2 teaspoons minced fresh thyme

3 cups chickpea flour or unbleached all-purpose flour

2 heaping tablespoons finely ground flaxseeds

2 cups unsweetened almond milk, homemade (page 152) or store-bought

2 cups panko breadcrumbs

Sunflower or safflower oil, for frying

3 tablespoons Creole Spice Blend (page 12)

4 small French sandwich rolls

Creamy Red Bell Pepper Sauce (page 136), for serving

2 cups shredded iceberg lettuce

2 heirloom tomatoes, cut into ¼-inch-thick slices

IN NEW ORLEANS, *a full-length po'boy is about one foot long, and a "shorty" is about six inches. Now I'm introducing a neologism for this three-inch version: lil' po'boy. I imagine these being served casually at a party, but you can always serve the six-inch version as a fun entrée along with a salad. These sandwiches are presented minimally, with iceberg lettuce and tomatoes as you would find on a traditional po'boy, and I dress them with a creamy roasted red bell pepper sauce to tame the spiciness of the tofu. For this recipe, I modified the tofu frying technique used by Bill Kim, the executive chef of BellyQ Restaurant in Chicago.*

Place each block of tofu on a long side and slice it in half lengthwise. Turn it onto the large side again, keeping the layers together, and slice crosswise into 3 even slabs. Cut each slab in half crosswise to yield 12 cubes per slab. Transfer the tofu to a large baking dish and spread it in a single layer.

To make the marinade, combine the water, tamari, orange juice, vinegar, lemon juice, garlic, and thyme in a blender and puree until smooth. Pour over the tofu and refrigerate for 6 hour or overnight, turning the tofu a few times to evenly coat with the marinade.

In a shallow dish, spread 1 cup of the flour. In a medium bowl, whisk together the flaxseeds, almond milk, and the remaining 2 cups flour. Spread the panko in another shallow dish. Dredge the tofu in the flour, the flaxseed mixture, and then the panko.

In a large saucepan, heat 1 inch of oil to 325°F. Fry the coated tofu cubes in batches, turning them until deep gold, about 7 minutes. Transfer to paper towels to drain and season with the spice blend.

As soon as the tofu is ready, split the rolls, leaving them attached at one edge. Spread a thin layer of red pepper sauce on both cut surfaces of each roll. Arrange 6 cubes of tofu on each sandwich. Top the tofu with the lettuce and tomatoes.

SWEET PLANTAIN and FRESH CORN CAKES

SWEET CORN, PLANTAIN, CORNMEAL, FLAXSEEDS

YIELD 24 cakes	**SOUNDTRACK** "Aaya Lolo" by The Barbecues from *Ghana Special: Modern Highlife, Afro Sounds & Ghanaian Blues 1968–81*

1 cup yellow cornmeal

¾ cup unbleached all-purpose flour

1½ teaspoons baking powder

½ teaspoon fine sea salt

1 tablespoon finely ground golden flaxseeds

2 cups plus 3 tablespoons unsweetened almond milk, homemade (page 152) or store-bought

1 overripe plantain, mashed

Kernels from 1 ear of sweet corn (store the cob in the freezer to make Corn Broth, page 43)

1 tablespoon extra-virgin olive oil, plus more as needed for panfrying

Salty Lemon Cream with Parsley (page 146), for serving

⅓ cup chopped fresh chives

IN OCTOBER 2012, *Alice Waters asked me to cook at a fundraiser for President Obama that she cohosted with Tyler Florence in San Francisco. I felt so honored to be making food with some of my favorite culinary creatives, including my neighbor Mary Canales and her business partner Mattea Soreng (Ici); my buddies Charlie Hallowell (Pizzaiolo) and Sylvan Mishima Brackett (Peko-Peko); and other stellar chefs, such as Russell Moore (Camino), Gayle Pirie and John Clark (Foreign Cinema), Charlene Reis and Paul Arenstam (Summer Kitchen), and Gilbert Pilgram and Annie Callan (Zuni Café).*

Chef Samantha Greenwood and I worked together to make tiny servings of my fresh corn cakes, and we served them topped with silken tofu cream and chopped chives. Inspired by tatale, fried plantain cakes traditional to Ghana, I've added mashed over-ripe plantains to this version for another slightly sweet layer of flavor that goes well with the corn. I recommend making these small and eating them as an appetizer with a dollop of Salty Lemon Cream with Parsley garnished with chives.

Put the cornmeal, flour, baking powder, and salt in a medium bowl and mix well. In a separate medium bowl, combine the flaxseeds and 3 tablespoons of the water and stir with a fork until well blended, about 30 seconds. Add the plantain and mash and mix with the fork until well incorporated. Stir in the remaining 2 cups water, then fold in the corn. Cover and refrigerate until cool and set, about 20 minutes.

Preheat the oven to 250°F.

Warm 1 tablespoon oil in a large cast-iron or nonstick skillet over medium-high heat. Spoon the batter into the pan, using 1 heaping tablespoon for each cake. Cook until golden on the bottom, 2 to 4 minutes. Gently turn and cook until the other side is golden, 2 to 4 minutes. Transfer the cooked cakes to a baking sheet and put them in the oven to keep warm until all the cakes are cooked. Serve them with the lemon cream garnished with the chives.

SKILLET CORNBREAD with PECAN DUKKAH

CORNMEAL, PECANS, SESAME SEEDS, CORIANDER, CUMIN

YIELD 16 servings as a snack, or 8 servings to accompany a meal

SOUNDTRACK "Wounds of Sorrow" by Arabian Knightz (featuring Sofia Baig) from *UKnighted State of Arabia*

1¾ cups yellow cornmeal

¼ cup unbleached all-purpose flour

1 teaspoon baking powder

1 teaspoon baking soda

¼ teaspoon fine sea salt

¼ cup Dukkah (recipe follows)

2 tablespoons finely ground golden flaxseeds

6 tablespoons water

1 cup unsweetened almond milk, homemade (page 152) or store-bought

¼ cup Creamed Cashews (page 143)

2 tablespoons apple cider vinegar

1 tablespoon finely grated orange zest

¼ cup coconut oil, melted, plus more for oiling

DUKKAH is an Egyptian mixture of nuts, seeds, and spices enjoyed throughout the Middle East and North Africa. From all available evidence, there is no standard recipe; Dukkah varies depending on ingredients available, region, and family. It's typically eaten as a snack or hors d'oeuvre on bread, by dipping the bread into olive oil then into the Dukkah. Therefore, I thought it would make a wonderful addition to skillet cornbread, a Southern staple. Of course, you can always make a streamlined version of this cornbread without the Dukkah. But once you make a batch of Dukkah, you can also sprinkle it on salads or vegetables for a burst of texture and flavor.

Although I initially imagined this cornbread being cut into small squares and served as a snack, it can certainly accompany a meal. In fact, I suggest having it with *Sweet Potato and Lima Bean Tagine* (page 57). I don't add any sugar to this recipe because authentic Southern cornbread typically doesn't include it, but I suppose you could add a tablespoon or two of raw cane sugar to the dry ingredients if you absolutely need a sweet element. This cornbread also makes fantastic croutons (recipe follows), which I like to serve along with my recipe for *Stewed Tomatoes and Black-Eyed Peas* (page 53).

Preheat the oven to 425°F.

Put the cornmeal, flour, baking powder, baking soda, salt, and *Dukkah* in a medium bowl and mix well. In a separate medium bowl, combine the flaxseeds and water and stir with a fork until well blended. Add the almond milk, cashew cream, vinegar, orange zest, and the ¼ cup oil and whisk until well blended.

Oil a 10-inch cast-iron skillet, then put it in the oven. After the skillet has heated for 3 minutes, pour the almond milk mixture into the cornmeal mixture and mix gently just until the dry ingredients are moist; don't overmix, or the texture of the cornbread will suffer. Remove the skillet from the oven and scrape the batter into it, spreading it in an even layer. Bake for about 20 minutes, until golden brown and firm to the touch, or until a skewer inserted in the center comes out clean. Cut into even pieces and serve hot.

{ continued }

DUKKAH

YIELD about ¹/₂ cup

7 tablespoons finely
   chopped pecans, toasted
   (see sidebar, page 119)
2 tablespoons black sesame
   seeds, toasted (see
   sidebar, page 119)

¹/₂ teaspoon coarse sea salt
2 teaspoons coriander seeds,
   toasted (see sidebar,
   page 9)
2 teaspoons cumin seeds,
   toasted (see sidebar,
   page 9)

Put the pecans, sesame seeds, and salt in a small bowl. Combine the coriander and cumin seeds in a mortar and pound with a pestle until smashed but not finely ground. Add to the pecans and mix well.

CORNBREAD CROUTONS

YIELD about 4 cups

1 recipe Skillet Cornbread,
   page 131
¹/₄ cup extra-virgin olive oil

To make cornbread croutons, preheat the oven to 350°F. Line a rimmed baking sheet with parchment paper.

Cut half of the pan of cornbread into 1-inch cubes; you should have about 28 pieces. Drizzle with the olive oil and toss gently. Transfer to the lined baking sheet and bake, shaking the pan every 5 minutes, for about 15 minutes, until the croutons are toasted.

PUMPKIN-PEANUT FRITTERS

PUMPKIN, PEANUTS

YIELD 4 to 6 servings

SOUNDTRACK "Leliyafu" by Ladysmith Black Mambazo from *Songs from a Zulu Farm*

¼ cup skinless raw peanuts

½ cup unbleached all-purpose flour

1 teaspoon baking powder

⅛ teaspoon fine sea salt

2 tablespoons finely ground golden flaxseeds

6 tablespoons water

1¾ cups pumpkin puree (see sidebar)

Coconut oil, for frying (about 3 cups)

PUMPKIN FRITTERS *are eaten in South Africa at breakfast or for dessert, but I think these make a perfect afternoon snack. My version has ground peanuts, which give the fritters more depth. While it might be tempting to use canned pumpkin puree, I suggest making your own to give your fritters the freshest taste possible.*

Place the peanuts in a mortar or in a plastic bag. Pound or crush the peanuts until finely ground. Transfer to a small bowl and stir in the flour, baking powder, and salt.

In a medium bowl, combine the flaxseeds and water and stir with a fork until well blended. Add the pumpkin puree and mix well. Add the flour mixture and beat with a wooden spoon until well combined, being careful not to overmix. Refrigerate for 5 minutes.

Preheat the oven to 200°F. Line a plate with paper towels.

Warm 1 inch of oil in a heavy medium saucepan until hot but not smoking, about 375°F. Working in batches of 5 fritters, carefully drop heaping tablespoons of the batter into the oil and fry, until browned, about 2 minutes. If the fritters are browning more quickly, decrease the temperature to prevent overcooking. Using a slotted spoon, transfer the fritters to the lined plate to drain, then transfer to a baking sheet and put them in the oven to keep warm until all the fritters are cooked. Serve hot.

MAKING PUMPKIN PUREE

Split a small pumpkin in half and scoop out the seeds. (Consider roasting them to eat as a snack, as described in the sidebar on page 119). Cut out the fibers. Put the pumpkin halves, cut side down, on a baking sheet and drizzle with a little olive oil. Bake at 400°F for about 45 minutes, until fork-tender. Scoop the pumpkin flesh into a food processor fitted with the metal blade and process until smooth, adding water if necessary. You can also use a blender, though you may need to add a little more water.

PRESERVES. CREAMS.
SPREADS.

I AM VERY EXCITED that more people are realizing the benefits of from-scratch home cooking: it's a powerful way to improve personal health since we have control over everything being put into our meals, it helps create a more sustainable planet when we use locally grown produce, and it allows us to save money since frequently eating outside the home can be expensive. My work celebrates this approach and encourages people to grow, prepare, and cook in community with others. In addition to saving money, time, energy, and resources when we grow food together, buy collectively in bulk, cook with a group of people, and share tools, we build connections with our family, friends, and neighbors.

As challenging as it may seem to be involved with our food from seed to table, it is important to remember that these practices reflect traditional ways of coming together. I strongly believe that we must go back to our roots in order to move forward (the concept of *sankofa*), and much of my work is rooted in the history and memories of my own family's connection to food. I grew up watching my maternal grandmother make everything from scratch in addition to canning, pickling, and preserving fruits and vegetables from her home garden in South Memphis, Tennessee. Although my grandparents are no longer here, I often have conversations with elders about living off the food that they grew on small farms and home gardens, canning and preserving, and sharing their bounty with their community.

I created the accompaniments in this chapter to be used with specific recipes in this book, but feel free to switch them up, as these flavor-enhancing recipes have a variety of uses. Spreads like Fig Preserves with Thyme (page 142), Maple-Plantain Spread (page 149), and Sweet Orange Blossom Cream (page 146) will liven up biscuits, cornbread, and cakes. Creamed Cashews (page 143) and Salty Lemon Cream with Parsley (page 146) add creaminess and thicken grains, soups, and stews. And Dill-Pickled Mustard Greens (page 138), Ginger-Pickled Green Beans (page 139), and Sweet Pickled Watermelon Rinds and Jalapeños (page 140) add crunch, color, and zest to a variety of meals.

CREAMY RED BELL PEPPER SAUCE

LEMON JUICE, RED WINE VINEGAR, TAMARI

| **YIELD** | **SOUNDTRACK** "Restless" by Kudu from *Kudu* |
| about 2 cups | |

1 red bell pepper, roasted (see sidebar), seeded, and cut into a few large slices

1 cup silken tofu

½ cup vegan mayonnaise

2 tablespoons extra-virgin olive oil

1 tablespoon freshly squeezed lemon juice

1 tablespoon red wine vinegar

1 tablespoon tamari

1 large clove garlic, minced

1 teaspoon paprika

¼ teaspoon coarse sea salt

¼ teaspoon freshly ground white pepper

½ teaspoon maple syrup

½ teaspoon Dijon mustard

I CREATED THIS SAUCE *specifically for Lil' Tofu Po'Boys (page 128), but it could be substituted for mayonnaise in almost any application.*

With a clean kitchen towel, pat the bell pepper slices dry. Put the pepper in a blender. Add the tofu, mayonnaise, oil, lemon juice, vinegar, tamari, garlic, paprika, salt, pepper, maple syrup, and mustard and process until smooth and creamy. Use immediately or store in a tightly sealed jar in the refrigerator for up to 1 week.

ROASTING PEPPERS AND CHILES

There are a few ways that I roast bell peppers and chiles: using a gas stove top, under a broiler, and on a grill.

If I'm roasting a single bell pepper, I tend to use a gas stove. Place the pepper directly on the burner with a low flame and turn frequently with tongs. Remove the pepper from the burner when most of the skin is blistered and blackened, place it in a bowl, and cover. Let the pepper cool for about 15 minutes, until you can handle it without burning your hands. Remove from the bowl and peel off the skin (do not wash the pepper or it will lose some of its flavor). Cut off the stem end, remove the core and seeds, and cut the pepper into strips, or use as directed in individual recipes. If not using immediately, place in a bowl, toss with a little bit of olive oil, and refrigerate until ready to use.

If roasting a larger quantity of peppers, I prefer to broil them. Place the peppers on a parchment paper–lined rimmed baking sheet and roast under a preheated broiler until they are blistered and blackened, 5 to 7 minutes, turning them a few times with tongs so they blacken evenly. Proceed as above.

If grilling, place the peppers directly on the grill grate and turn them frequently with tongs. Remove them from the grill when most of the skin is blistered and blackened, then proceed as above.

CUMIN-PICKLED ONIONS

WHITE VINEGAR, RAW CANE SUGAR, CUMIN, BLACK PEPPERCORNS

YIELD
about 2 cups

SOUNDTRACK "The Blessing" by Ornette Coleman from *Something Else!!!!*

½ cup apple cider vinegar

1½ cups water

1 tablespoon raw cane sugar

1 teaspoon cumin seeds toasted (see sidebar, page 9)

1 teaspoon black peppercorns

2 red onions, sliced into thin rings

A SIMPLE RECIPE *for sandwich-worthy onions. Try them on the Berbere-Spiced Black-Eyed Pea Sliders (page 32).*

Put the vinegar, water, sugar, cumin, and peppercorns in a medium saucepan and bring to a boil over medium-high heat. Decrease the heat to medium and cook, stirring occasionally, until the sugar dissolves, about 5 minutes. Remove from the heat and let cool to room temperature.

Put the onions in a canning jar, then pour the vinegar mixture into the jar. Cover tightly and refrigerate for at least 1 day before eating. Stored in the refrigerator, the onions will keep for up to 1 month.

DILL-PICKLED MUSTARD GREENS

APPLE CIDER VINEGAR, DILL SEEDS, BLACK PEPPERCORNS, FRESH DILL, SERRANO CHILE, GARLIC

YIELD	SOUNDTRACK *"Green Eyed Love"* (Waajeed Remix) by Mayer Hawthorne from *Green Eyed Love Remixes*
about 2 cups	

½ cup apple cider
    vinegar

1½ cups water

1 tablespoon plus
    2 teaspoons coarse
    sea salt

1 teaspoon dill seeds

1 teaspoon black
    peppercorns

2 pounds mustard greens

2 tablespoons chopped
    fresh dill

2 serrano chiles, thinly
    sliced

1 clove garlic

THESE MUSTARD GREENS *are great for adding a tangy element to any meal. After creating a recipe for Quick-Pickled Mustard Greens for* The Inspired Vegan *for use as a sweet pickled condiment, I wanted to make a savory version. Use this on sandwiches, in stews, and in vegetables dishes that would benefit from a tangy and savory element.*

Put the vinegar, water, 2 teaspoons of the salt, the dill seeds, and the peppercorns in a medium saucepan. Cook over high heat, stirring often, until the salt has dissolved, about 3 minutes. Remove from the heat.

Put about 12 cups of water in a large pot and bring to a boil over high heat. While the water is heating up, strip the leaves of the mustard greens from their stems. Thinly slice the stems and set aside. Coarsely chop the leaves.

When the water is boiling, add the remaining 1 tablespoon salt, then add the mustard stems and cook uncovered for 1 minute. Remove from the heat, add the mustard leaves, and let sit for 1 minute. Drain in a colander and rinse with cool water to stop the cooking. Press the greens to extract as much liquid as possible.

Transfer the greens and stems to a 1-pint or large canning jar and add the dill, chiles, and garlic. Pour in the vinegar mixture and let cool to room temperature. Cover tightly and refrigerate for at least 1 day before eating. Stored in the refrigerator, the greens will keep for up to 1 month.

GINGER-PICKLED GREEN BEANS

GREEN BEANS, GINGER, WHITE VINEGAR, RAW CANE SUGAR

YIELD 3 pints	**SOUNDTRACK** "Green Lights" by Aloe Blacc from *Good Things*

1 pound green beans, trimmed and cut into 4-inch pieces

3 tablespoons minced fresh ginger

2 cups white vinegar

2 cups water

3 tablespoons raw cane sugar

1 tablespoon coarse sea salt

PICKLED GREEN BEANS *are a staple on Southern tables, but I rarely see them in Northern California. Then, out of nowhere, I saw them on the starter menu of a restaurant in San Francisco. Although I don't recall the restaurant, I definitely recall the beans. They were so tasty that I had to come up with my own version. After seeing Hugh Acheson's recipe for gingered pickled carrots in A New Turn in the South, I decided to add ginger to my pickled green beans for subtle spiciness. (Pictured on page 141.)*

Divide the green beans among three 1-pint canning jars and add 1 tablespoon of the ginger to each jar.

Put the vinegar, water, sugar, and salt in a medium saucepan. Cook over medium-high heat, stirring occasionally, until the sugar and salt have dissolved, about 3 minutes. Divide the liquid among the jars, leaving 1/2 inch of headspace in each jar. Cover tightly and refrigerate for at least 1 day before eating. Stored in the refrigerator, the beans will keep for up to 1 month.

SWEET PICKLED WATERMELON RINDS and JALAPEÑOS

WHITE VINEGAR, RAW CANE SUGAR, NAVEL ORANGE, LEMON

YIELD	SOUNDTRACK "Litorânea" by Clara Moreno (featuring Celso Fonseca) from *Clara Moreno*
6 pints	

Rind from a medium watermelon (a 10- to 12-pound melon)

2 cups thinly sliced jalapeño chiles

3 cups water

3 cups raw cane sugar

2 teaspoons coarse sea salt

2 large navel oranges with peel, thinly sliced

4 lemons with peel, thinly sliced

2 cups white vinegar

DON'T GET RID OF *those watermelon rinds just yet! Pickling is a great way to make the most of them. While pickled watermelon rinds were fairly common in the South, these are unique in that I add jalapeños for a subtle kick. The rinds are great alongside savory dishes, similar to how you'd use chutney. You can cut them into thin slices and eat them on Berbere-Spiced Black-Eyed Pea Sliders (page 32) for another layer of flavor on that burger.*

Sterilize six 1-pint canning jars and their lids.

Prepare the watermelon rinds by removing the green skin with a Y-shaped peeler or utility knife and cutting away most of the red flesh with a knife (leaving just a thin coat), while keeping the rinds as thick as possible. Cut as much of the rind as possible into 1-inch cubes, though, obviously, many of the pieces will be odd shapes, until you have 10 cups of prepared rind.

Put the rinds in a large pot and add water to cover. Bring to a boil over high heat. Decrease the heat to medium, cover, and simmer until just fork-tender but still firm, 8 to 10 minutes. Drain well and set aside until cool. (No need to clean the pot.)

Divide the watermelon rinds evenly among the sterilized jars, then distribute the jalapeños evenly among the jars.

Put the water, sugar, and salt in the same pot and bring to a boil over high heat. Decrease the heat to medium and cook, stirring often, until the sugar and salt have dissolved.

Divide the orange and lemon slices evenly among the sterilized jars, then immediately pour in the hot vinegar mixture, dividing it evenly among the jars. Stored in the refrigerator, the pickles should keep for a few months.

FIG PRESERVES with THYME

MISSION FIGS, RAW CANE SUGAR, LEMON JUICE

YIELD 4 to 5 pints | **SOUNDTRACK** "Summer Sun" (Markus Enochson Remix) by Koop from *Waltz for Koop—Alternative Takes*

4 pounds just-ripe Mission figs, stemmed and quartered lengthwise

1 cup water

1½ cups raw cane sugar

2 tablespoons freshly squeezed lemon juice

4 sprigs thyme

MY FRIEND *Shakirah Simley created this recipe especially for this book. She's the owner of Slow Jams and also works as the community coordinator for the Bi-Rite Family of Businesses in San Francisco, which includes two grocery stores, an ice cream shop, and a combination art gallery and community space. Shakirah notes that Mission figs work best for this jam and suggests looking for fruit with purplish black skin, pink flesh, and slight splits, with a bit of nectar on the stem as an indication of perfect ripeness and juiciness. This spread was created for storing in the refrigerator and giving away to friends, so no need to go through the process of sealing them.*

Sterilize five 1-pint canning jars and their lids.

Put all the ingredients in a large heavy pot over medium heat. Cook, stirring gently, until the sugar is dissolved. Increase the heat to medium-high and bring to a boil. Cook, stirring constantly, until thickened, 10 to 12 minutes (see the note for a doneness test). Remove from the heat. Discard the thyme. Ladle the jam into the sterilized jars. Stored in the refrigerator, the jam will keep for 6 months.

NOTE: To determine if the jam is done, Shakirah offers this "cold plate test": Before making the jam, put a couple plates in the freezer. Get them really cold. To test doneness, put a spoonful of hot jam on a cold plate. Wait a minute, then run a finger through the middle of the jam blob. If the two sides stay separate, it's ready! If not, cook a little longer and test again.

CREAMED CASHEWS

CASHEWS

YIELD
about 1 cup

SOUNDTRACK "Quicksand" by J*Davey from *Evil Christian Cop*

1 cup raw cashews, soaked in water overnight and drained well

½ cup water

ALTHOUGH NATIVE TO northeastern Brazil, the majority of cashews sold in North America come from India and East Africa. In fact, according to the Food and Agriculture Organization of the United Nations, Nigeria was the world's largest producer of cashew nuts in 2010. A lot of people are not aware that cashew nuts come from the bottom of the pear-shaped cashew apple, a refreshing fruit that is eaten widely in the Caribbean and Brazil. People also enjoy the juice of cashew apples as a refreshing drink. Cashews are important in Brazilian cuisine and used in a variety of dishes. My Creamy Coconut-Cashew Soup with Okra, Corn, and Tomatoes (page 48) is a nod to vatapá, a popular Brazilian stew. Soaking cashews and then pureeing them with water in a blender creates a rich, smooth dairy-free substitute for heavy cream that gives dishes a creamy consistency and more depth. I also use it in fruit smoothies to add protein and make them creamier. Note: Look for whole cashews that are white and crisp.

Put the cashews and water in a blender and process until smooth and creamy. Use immediately or store in a covered container the refrigerator for up to 4 days.

SALTY LEMON CREAM with PARSLEY

OLIVE OIL, LEMON JUICE, LEMON ZEST, DIJON MUSTARD, SEA SALT

YIELD
about 1 cup

SOUNDTRACK "Slide" by Slave from *Slave*

4 tablespoons packed chopped flat-leaf parsley

1 cup firm silken tofu

Finely grated zest of 1 lemon

2 tablespoons freshly squeezed lemon juice

1 tablespoon extra-virgin olive oil

½ teaspoon Dijon mustard

1 large clove garlic, minced

½ teaspoon coarse sea salt

THIS IS A TOFU-BASED CREAM *that you can use like sour cream or crème fraîche. I've experimented with several brands of silken tofu for this recipe, and I find that the Mori-Nu brand works best.*

Set aside 2 tablespoons of the parsley. Put the remaining parsley in a blender. Add the tofu, lemon zest, lemon juice, oil, mustard, garlic, and salt and blend until creamy. Transfer to a bowl. Mince the reserved parsley and stir it in. Season with salt to taste, cover, and refrigerate for at least 1 hour before serving. Stored in the refrigerator, it will keep for 3 days.

SWEET ORANGE BLOSSOM CREAM

NAVEL ORANGE, ORANGE BLOSSOM WATER, BOURBON, AGAVE NECTAR

YIELD
about 1 cup

SOUNDTRACK "All 4 You" by Om'mas Keith (featuring Erykah Badu) from *City Pulse*

1 cup firm silken tofu

Finely grated zest of 1 navel orange

¼ cup freshly squeezed navel orange juice

¼ cup agave nectar

1 tablespoon bourbon

1 teaspoon fine sea salt

1 teaspoon orange blossom water

I CAME UP *with this recipe with sweet breakfast dishes and desserts in mind. It's wonderful with Maple-Glazed Banana Johnnycakes (page 156), Date-Almond Cornbread Muffins (page 157), or Spiced Persimmon Bundt Cake with Orange Glaze (page 176).*

Put all the ingredients in a blender and process until smooth and creamy. Cover and refrigerate until chilled, at least 1 hour. Stored in the refrigerator, it will keep for up to 3 days.

START WITH A MEAL

In order to collectively build power and generate solutions for fixing our broken food system, more people need to be aware of the issues. Malcolm X once said, "The greatest mistake of the movement has been trying to organize a sleeping people around specific goals. You have to wake the people up first, then you'll get action." For the past fifty years, most Americans have been lulled to sleep by billions of dollars spent influencing them to eat a lot of food that is harmful to their health and by food policy designed to boost the profits of big agribusiness.

While it is becoming increasingly clear to more and more Americans that our food system is broken and that we need to collectively do something to fix it, many people simply aren't aware of the structurally based threats to public health and the foundations of our food system. Through cookbook writing, I strive to open the door for more people to have pleasurable experiences with wholesome, fresh food, which I believe is a revolutionary first step toward food justice.

I've said it once, and I will say it one thousand times more: Start with the visceral, move to the cerebral, and end with the political. We don't have to eat food that's replete with pesticides, antibiotics, and growth hormones. We don't have to eat produce that's been shipped across the country or the globe and that tastes like cardboard. We don't have to shop at supersized big-box stores to get food that many of us can just as easily obtain from local small farms. We can come together as a nation and vote with our dollars, voices, and ballots for a different food system for our children, grandchildren, and generations to come. And we can start by making a meal.

MANGO-MAPLE SYRUP

MANGO, LEMON ZEST, LEMON JUICE, APPLE CIDER VINEGAR

YIELD
about 1 cup

SOUNDTRACK "Banana" by Madlib & Joyce Moreno (featuring Generation Match) from *Red Hot + Rio 2*

½ cup Grade B maple syrup

½ cup diced ripe mango

¼ cup water

1 tablespoon freshly squeezed lemon juice

2 teaspoons apple cider vinegar

1 teaspoon finely grated lemon zest

Pinch of fine sea salt

I ORIGINALLY MADE *this maple syrup with a tropical twist as an accompaniment for my Maple-Glazed Banana Johnnycakes (page 156) and have since found that the syrup goes well with a number of bready breakfast treats. No need to use a lot, as it is deliciously sweet.*

Put all the ingredients in a small saucepan over low heat and bring to a simmer. Cook, stirring occasionally, until the mango is falling apart, about 15 minutes. Let cool, then transfer to a blender and process until creamy. Strain through a fine-mesh sieve into a 1-pint glass jar, pressing the solids to extract as much liquid as possible. Use immediately, or seal tightly and store in the refrigerator for up to 2 weeks.

MAPLE-PLANTAIN SPREAD

MAPLE SYRUP, LEMON JUICE, LEMON ZEST, ORANGE JUICE, BOURBON

YIELD
about 2 cups

SOUNDTRACK "Butter" by A Tribe Called Quest from *The Low End Theory*

1 large ripe plantain (about 12 ounces), chopped

¾ cup water

½ cup Grade B maple syrup

1 teaspoon coconut oil

2 tablespoons freshly squeezed orange juice

¼ teaspoon finely grated lemon zest

2 teaspoons freshly squeezed lemon juice

½ teaspoon bourbon

Scant ¼ teaspoon fine sea salt

I ORIGINATED *this recipe as an accompaniment for my Teff Biscuits (page 158), to provide both the creaminess of butter and the sweetness of a fruit spread. It's also delicious on toast. It congeals a bit when refrigerated, so bring it to room temperature and whip it with a spoon right before serving. If a plantain is not available, you could use a just-ripe banana instead.*

Put all the ingredients in a small saucepan and bring to a boil over high heat. Decrease the heat to medium and simmer, stirring often, until the plantains are soft and the liquid is thickening, about 10 minutes. Let cool for 5 minutes.

Transfer to a blender and process until creamy, scraping down the sides if necessary. Transfer to a bowl, cover, and refrigerate until chilled, about 30 minutes. Serve at room temperature. Stored in the refrigerator, it will keep for 5 days.

BISCUITS. SMOOTHIES. PORRIDGE.

ONE OF THE MOST important meals of my family's day is breakfast. When I was single and childless I would sometimes wake up, dive into a project, and get so preoccupied that I didn't eat, or even drink, until it was time for lunch. Having a daughter has helped me be much more mindful about eating something soon after I get out of bed. Knowing that my two-year-old's growing body and developing brain are negatively impacted if she doesn't have adequate nutrition to start her day has helped me consider how skipping meals can be harmful to my own physical and intellectual well-being, as well as my mood. (Just ask my wife how grumpy I am when I haven't eaten.) Simply put, I now know that starting my day with a good breakfast provides me with a much needed nutritional boost that gives me energy throughout the day, prevents me from overeating at lunch, and helps me be more alert and happy!

As with other meals, I try to let the seasons guide what I eat for breakfast. During the late fall and winter, I often have warming bowls of oatmeal, porridge, or congee. In the spring and summer, I have granola, fresh fruit, coconut milk yogurt, and smoothies. Most weekdays my breakfasts are pretty simple, but on Saturdays and Sundays I often bake bread, fry johnnycakes, and cook full meals with both sweet and savory elements. The dishes in this chapter are fun and nourishing, and I provide a variety of options, from quick morning snacks to leisurely weekend brunches.

For a quick on-the-go meal, you can't go wrong with a Fresh Peach, Banana, and Warm Millet Smoothie (page 155) or Date-Almond Cornbread Muffins (page 157). Filled with bananas, blueberries, and coconut water, a glass of Purp 2.0 (page 153) is both hydrating and replenishing and serves as a perfect after-workout drink. Millet and Sweet Potato Porridge (page 162) will provide a warming and filling start to your day, and Fresh Corn Grits with Swiss Chard and Roasted Cherry Tomatoes (page 160) will take your summer brunch to the next level.

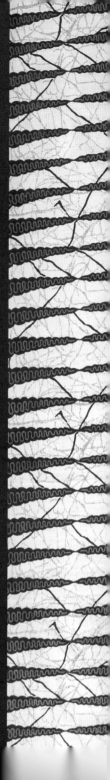

DATE-SWEETENED ALMOND MILK

ALMONDS, DATES, ORANGE BLOSSOM WATER

YIELD about 4 cups ‖ **SOUNDTRACK** "Free" by Malika Zarra from *On the Ebony Road*

1½ cups raw almonds, blanched (see sidebar), soaked in water overnight, and drained well

3½ cups water

4 Medjool dates, pitted and chopped

1 teaspoon orange blossom water

Pinch of fine sea salt

ALMOND MILK isn't just some hippie replacement for cow's milk, as Rosamund Grant and Josephine Bacon explain in their cookbook The Taste of Africa: "Almond milk has been a favourite beverage since medieval times, when it was valued because it could be made as needed and did not sour like the dairy product." Because 75 percent of African-Americans are lactose intolerant and don't digest milk well, I included a recipe for almond milk in Vegan Soul Kitchen, but this one is slightly different. Inspired by Grant and Bacon's recipe in The Taste of Africa, I've added orange blossom water to give it a North African twist.

This version can be served cold or almost frozen as a refreshing treat. I also call for fresh almond milk in several recipes in this book. If using it for a savory recipe, omit the dates and orange blossom water. To make other varieties of nondairy milk, experiment with substituting different raw nuts and seeds to see which ones are tasty to you and your family.

Put all the ingredients in a blender and process until smooth. Strain through a piece of cheesecloth into a pitcher, squeezing the cheesecloth to extract as much liquid as possible. Stored in the refrigerator, it should last 5 days.

BLANCHING ALMONDS

Put the almonds in a heatproof bowl and pour in boiling water to cover. After 1 minute, drain the almonds in a colander, then rinse them with cold water. Drain well, transfer to a clean kitchen towel, and pat dry. Use your fingers to slip off the skins.

PURP 2.0

COCONUT WATER, BLUEBERRIES, BANANA, CASHEWS, ORANGE JUICE, LEMON JUICE

YIELD 2 generous servings	**SOUNDTRACK** "30,000 Feet" by The MASTRS from *Green EP*	**BOOK** *After Artest: The NBA and the Assault on Blackness* by David J. Leonard

6 tablespoons raw cashews, soaked in water overnight and drained well

1¼ cups coconut water, chilled

1 cup fresh blueberries, plus a few for garnish

1 ripe banana, frozen

6 tablespoons freshly squeezed orange juice

2 tablespoons freshly squeezed lemon juice

1 tablespoon finely ground golden flaxseeds

1 teaspoon maca powder (optional)

⅛ teaspoon ground cinnamon

THIS SMOOTHIE *is my tongue-in-cheek all-natural answer to sizzurp, a narcotic drink with origins in Houston, Texas, popularized by Southern hip-hop artists. Also known as lean, water, and purple drank, sizzurp is a combination of prescription cough syrup with codeine and some type of sugary soft drink. In 2012, rapper Lil Wayne spent several days in the intensive care unit of a Los Angeles hospital after a series of seizures, and many people speculated that his health was being negatively impacted by his excessive consumption of purple drank.*

Purp 2.0 is pretty straightforward. Nutrient-packed blueberries, potassium-filled bananas, and hydrating coconut water (also full of potassium) coalesce to form a visually appealing, health-supporting, and delicious smoothie. Soaked cashews plus fresh lemon juice and orange juice give it a tangy creaminess similar to that of yogurt. Ground flaxseeds (native to Egypt) add additional minerals, antioxidants, and vitamins, and if you really want to get crunk, add maca (a Peruvian root purported to boost energy, improve mood, and increase libido). Just make sure to drink it immediately, as it loses its attractive color after a few minutes.

Put the cashews and coconut water in a blender and process until smooth, about 2 minutes. Add the blueberries, banana, orange juice, lemon juice, flaxseeds, maca powder, and cinnamon and process until smooth. Serve garnished with a few blueberries.

FRESH PEACH, BANANA, and WARM MILLET SMOOTHIE

ORANGE JUICE, LIME JUICE, DATES, CASHEWS

YIELD 2 generous servings, or 4 smaller servings

SOUNDTRACK "Jambo Bwana" by Samba Salad from *Kids World Party*

2 tablespoons millet

2 cups water

Pinch of coarse sea salt

2 cups finely diced peeled peaches

2 large ripe bananas

1 cup freshly squeezed orange juice

¼ cup raw cashews, soaked in water overnight and drained well

2 Medjool dates, pitted

2 teaspoons freshly squeezed lime juice

FRUITY, WARM, and *filling, this drink always leaves me thoroughly satisfied. The idea for it came from a visit to the Raleigh-Durham area a few years ago. I was there to give a talk, and one of my buddies from college, Njathi Kabui, came to hear my presentation. I hadn't seen him in over a decade and discovered that he was the founder and executive chef of Organics and Sound, a company that provides education about healthy eating highlighted by site-specific dining events that bring together local food, music, art, and community.*

That evening we invited a few people over for a dinner inspired by the cuisine of Kabui's homeland, Kenya, and stayed up late discussing food, politics, and black folks. The next morning, he warmed up some leftover millet from the night before and pureed it in a blender with orange juice and fresh fruit. After drinking the smoothie, I was full and felt energized for the rest of the morning. Similar to Kabui's concoction, this is the perfect on-the-go smoothie.

Drinking a standard fruit smoothie is a great way to stay hydrated and contribute to your recommended daily consumption of fruit, but adding protein-packed ancient grains like millet, quinoa, and amaranth makes this a power smoothie. Ideally, you'd use leftover millet and simply warm it before blending, but I've included directions for cooking a small amount to use in your smoothie. You can also drink it cold; simply cook millet the night before (if not using leftovers) and add ½ cup of ice. Whether you drink it warm or cold, enjoy sipping it while dancing around and jumping up and down to one of my daughter's favorite songs, "Jambo Bwana."

Combine the millet and 1 cup of the water in a small saucepan and refrigerate overnight. In the morning, stir in the salt and bring to a boil over medium heat. Immediately decrease the heat to low, cover, and simmer until most of the liquid is absorbed, about 20 minutes. Remove from the heat and let sit, covered, for about 10 minutes.

Put 1½ cups of the peaches and the bananas, orange juice, cashews, dates, lime juice, and the remaining 1 cup water in a blender and process until smooth. Scrape in the millet and any cooking liquid and puree until smooth. Serve garnished with the remaining peaches.

MAPLE-GLAZED BANANA JOHNNYCAKES

CORNMEAL, BANANAS, FLAXSEEDS, PECANS

YIELD 12 to 14 cakes; 4 to 6 servings

SOUNDTRACK "Sunshine" by Audiopharmacy from *U Forgot About Us*

1 tablespoon plus 2 teaspoons coconut oil, plus more as needed for panfrying

5 tablespoons maple syrup

½ teaspoon ground cinnamon

3 cups diced just-ripe bananas

1½ cups yellow cornmeal

½ cup whole wheat pastry flour

2 tablespoons finely ground golden flaxseeds

1 teaspoon baking powder

1 teaspoon fine sea salt

2½ cups Date-Sweetened Almond Milk (page 152)

½ cup pecans, toasted (see sidebar, page 119) and chopped

Mango-Maple Syrup (page 148) and Sweet Orange Blossom Cream (page 146), for serving

JOHNNYCAKES, *flat cornmeal cakes popular in the South, are thought to be America's first flatbread, as they were a staple food of Native Americans. Here I interpret them as dense pancakes. These are great for breakfast on the weekend. I suggest eating them with Mango-Maple Syrup and Sweet Orange Blossom Cream, but because the johnny-cakes are sweetened by the maple-glazed bananas, you need only a little of both.*

Put 2 teaspoons of the oil and the maple syrup and cinnamon in a medium skillet and cook over medium heat, stirring occasionally, until simmering. Add the bananas and cook, stirring often, until soft, 2 to 3 minutes. Remove from the heat.

Put the cornmeal, flour, flaxseeds, baking powder, and salt in a large bowl and mix well.

Put the almond milk in a small saucepan and bring to a simmer over medium-high heat. Slowly pour it into the cornmeal mixture while stirring constantly. With a slotted spoon, lift the bananas from the skillet and add to the batter. Gently fold in, then cover and refrigerate for 20 minutes.

Preheat the oven to 250°F.

Warm the remaining 1 tablespoon oil in a large nonstick skillet or griddle over medium-high heat. Portion the batter into the skillet, using a little more than ¼ cup batter per cake. A large skillet should comfortably fit 2 or 3 cakes without touching. After about 1 minute, when the bottom starts to set, decrease the heat to medium-low and use a wooden spoon to shape the cakes, pushing them in and up so they are about 3 inches wide and ½ inch thick. Cook until golden brown and crispy on the bottom, 8 to 10 minutes. Flip the cakes, add a bit more oil, and tilt the pan to distribute the oil evenly. Cook until golden brown and crispy on the other side, 8 to 10 more minutes. Transfer the cakes to a baking sheet and put them in the oven to keep warm until all the cakes are cooked.

Serve with the pecans, syrup, and orange blossom cream alongside for topping.

DATE-ALMOND CORNBREAD MUFFINS

DATES, ALMONDS, CORNMEAL, ORANGE BLOSSOM WATER

YIELD	SOUNDTRACK "You'll Never Walk Alone" by Aretha Franklin from *Amazing Grace: The Complete Recordings*	BOOK *Looking for Leroy: Illegible Black Masculinities* by Mark Anthony Neal
9 muffins		

½ cup pitted Medjool dates

3 tablespoons coconut oil, plus more for oiling

¾ cup yellow cornmeal

¾ cup unbleached all-purpose flour

2 tablespoons raw cane sugar

1 tablespoon baking powder

½ teaspoon ground cinnamon

½ teaspoon fine sea salt

2 heaping tablespoons finely ground golden flaxseeds

6 tablespoons water

1 cup Date-Sweetened Almond Milk (page 152)

1 tablespoon orange blossom water

½ cup blanched almond slivers, toasted (see sidebar, page 119)

INSPIRED BY the sweet corn muffins that my paw paw used to make with Jiffy mix, as well as dates and almonds, which are often found in North African cuisine, these tasty muffins are one of my favorite breakfast treats. Creamy pureed Medjool dates add moisture and sweetness, and the combination of nutty cornmeal and almond slivers gives these hearty muffins satisfying crunch. Though it's subtle, the orange blossom water adds a sweet floral note that lingers after each bite. The muffins are terrific alone, but when paired with Sweet Orange Blossom Cream (page 146), they're superb; simply omit the orange blossom water and reduce the agave nectar by half in that recipe. This batter would also make tasty waffles. Note: this recipe is designed to yield nine plump muffins, so choose your muffin tin accordingly.

Preheat the oven to 400°F.

Put the dates in a small heatproof bowl and add boiling water to cover. Let soak for about 5 minutes.

Drain the dates, reserving the liquid, and put them in a food processor fitted with the metal blade. Add 1 tablespoon of the reserved soaking liquid and process until mostly creamy but with a few small chunks remaining, scraping down the sides and adding more of the reserved soaking liquid if necessary.

Generously coat 9 cups of a standard muffin tin with coconut oil, then put it in the oven.

Sift the cornmeal, flour, sugar, baking powder, cinnamon, and salt into a large bowl and stir with a whisk until well blended.

Put the flaxseeds and water in a medium bowl and whisk until well blended. Add the almond milk, oil, and orange blossom water and whisk until well combined. Pour into the cornmeal mixture and stir a few times with a large spoon, just until combined. Fold in the almonds, then fold in the date puree.

Remove the muffin tin from the oven. Scrape the batter into the 9 oiled muffin cups, distributing it evenly among them. They should be a little over three-quarters full. Bake for about 17 minutes, until golden brown.

Let cool in the tin for about 10 minutes, then transfer to a rack to cool a bit more. Serve warm.

TEFF BISCUITS with MAPLE-PLANTAIN SPREAD

TEFF FLOUR, COCONUT OIL, ALMOND MILK, CINNAMON

YIELD	SOUNDTRACK "Yèkatit (February)" by Mulatu Astatke from Éthiopiques, Volume 4: Ethio Jazz & Musique Instrumentale 1969–1974	BOOK To 'Joy My Freedom: Southern Black Women's Lives and Labors after the Civil War by Tera W. Hunter
5 servings		

1¼ cups unbleached all-purpose flour

¾ cup teff flour

1 tablespoon raw cane sugar

2 teaspoons baking powder

¾ teaspoon fine sea salt

½ teaspoon baking soda

7 tablespoons coconut oil, chilled, plus melted coconut oil, for brushing (optional)

1 cup cold Date-Sweetened Almond Milk (page 152)

1 tablespoon apple cider vinegar

Maple-Plantain Spread (page 149) or Fig Preserves with Thyme (page 142), for serving

NOTHING SAYS Southern breakfast like hot-out-of-the-oven biscuits. I have fond memories of sopping up maple syrup, molasses, and sorghum syrup with my maternal grandmother's homemade biscuits, and I often visualize her standing at her kitchen counter rolling out biscuit dough. For me, her practice of making biscuits almost every weekend has come to symbolize the hospitality, rituals, and slow-food traditions of African-American cookery that I'm hoping to help revive with my work.

To give these biscuits an East African twist, I use teff flour, made from a grain native to Ethiopia. Teff is one of the most nutritious grains in the world. It has the highest calcium content of any grain, and it's a good source of vitamin C and iron. I have no doubt that you'll will be making these biscuits often, as they're irresistible when split open and slathered with creamy, sweet Maple-Plantain Spread or my friend Shakirah's Fig Preserves with Thyme.

Preheat the oven to 425°F.

Sift the flours, sugar, baking powder, salt, and baking soda into a large bowl and stir with a whisk until well blended. Add the coconut oil and use 2 butter knives to cut it in until the mixture is the size of small peas. Put the almond milk and vinegar in a small bowl and stir well. Make a well in the center of the flour mixture and pour in the almond milk. Stir just until the dough comes away from the sides of the bowl.

Lightly dust a work surface with flour. Turn the dough out onto the work surface and knead 6 to 8 times. With floured hands, pat the dough into a ½-inch-thick disk.

With a floured 3-inch round cutter, cut out biscuits and put them on 2 large plates. Put in the freezer for 5 minutes or in the refrigerator for 15 minutes to chill. For a deeper golden color when baked, brush the tops lightly with melted coconut oil. Transfer to a large baking sheet and bake for 16 to 18 minutes, until golden.

Cool slightly, then split open with a butter knife and slather on some Maple-Plantain Spread.

FRESH CORN GRITS with SWISS CHARD and ROASTED CHERRY TOMATOES

GRITS, CASHEWS, PARSLEY

YIELD 4 to 6 servings

SOUNDTRACK "Solace" by Scott Joplin from *The Entertainer*

BOOK *The New Jim Crow: Mass Incarceration in the Age of Colorblindness* by Michelle Alexander

2 pounds cherry tomatoes, quartered

1 tablespoon plus 2 teaspoons extra-virgin olive oil

1 tablespoon plus 1³/₄ teaspoons coarse sea salt

12 ounces Swiss chard, stemmed and cut into bite-size pieces

Kernels from 2 large ears of sweet corn (store the cobs in the freezer to make Corn Broth, page 43)

¹/₂ cup finely diced yellow onion

1 large clove garlic, minced

4¹/₄ cups water

³/₄ cup yellow corn grits

¹/₂ cup Creamed Cashews (page 143)

1 teaspoon red wine vinegar

Freshly ground black pepper

¹/₄ cup packed minced flat-leaf parsley

WARM, CREAMY, AND COLORFUL, *this hearty dish would be a welcome addition to any summer brunch, but I created it with a Juneteenth sweet and savory brunch in mind. Juneteenth (June 19th), also known as Emancipation Day and Freedom Day, is the oldest known celebration commemorating the ending of slavery in the United States. On January 1, 1980, Juneteenth became an official state holiday in Texas through the efforts of Al Edwards, an African-American state legislator, and it is now recognized as a state holiday or state holiday observance in forty-two states.*

Preheat the oven to 400°F. Line a large, rimmed baking sheet with parchment paper.

Put the tomatoes in a large bowl, drizzle with the 1 tablespoon of the oil, and sprinkle with ¹/₂ teaspoon of the salt. Toss gently until the tomatoes are evenly coated. Transfer to the lined baking sheet and spread in a single layer. Bake for about 30 minutes, until the tomato skins begin to brown.

Meanwhile, put about 12 cups of water in a large pot and bring to a boil over high heat. Add 1 tablespoon of the salt, then add the chard and cook uncovered for 1 minute. With a skimmer or slotted spoon, transfer the chard to a colander, pressing to extract as much liquid as possible, then transfer to a cutting board. Remove the boiling water from the heat, add the corn, and let sit for 1 minute. Drain the corn. Finely chop the chard.

Heat the remaining 2 teaspoons oil in a medium sauté pan over medium heat. Add the onion and ¹/₄ teaspoon of the salt and sauté until the onion is soft, 5 to 7 minutes. Add the garlic and sauté until the garlic is fragrant, 2 to 3 minutes. Stir in the chard and ¹/₄ cup of the water. Cover and simmer until the chard is tender, 3 to 5 minutes.

Put 3 cups of the water and the remaining 1 teaspoon salt in a medium saucepan and bring to a boil over medium-high heat. Slowly pour in the grits, whisking constantly until no lumps remain. Return to a boil, then immediately decrease the heat to low. Simmer uncovered, whisking occasionally, until the grits have absorbed most of the liquid and are beginning to thicken, 3 to 5 minutes. Add the remaining 1 cup water and simmer, whisking occasionally, until most of the liquid has been absorbed, about 10 minutes. Stir in the cashew cream, cover, and simmer, whisking frequently, until the grits are soft and fluffy, about 30 minutes. Fold in the reserved corn. The grits should be thick yet creamy. Add a bit of water to thin them if necessary.

Drizzle the vinegar over the tomatoes and toss gently to combine. Serve the grits topped with the greens, a few grinds of black pepper, and a tablespoon or two of the tomatoes, lifting them out of their juices with a slotted spoon, for a bit of fruity acidity. Garnish with the parsley.

MILLET and SWEET POTATO PORRIDGE

ALMOND MILK, CASHEWS, MOLASSES, MAPLE SYRUP, PECANS

YIELD 4 to 6 servings

SOUNDTRACK "Black Voices" (5:49 version) by Tony Allen from *Black Voices*

BOOK *Soledad Brother: The Prison Letters of George Jackson* by George Jackson

1 small sweet potato (about 8 ounces)

½ cup millet, soaked in water overnight and drained well

2 cups water

1 (2-inch) cinnamon stick

1 cup unsweetened almond milk, homemade (see page 152) or store-bought, plus more for serving

¼ cup Creamed Cashews (page 143)

2 teaspoons unsulfured molasses

2 teaspoons maple syrup, plus more for serving

½ teaspoon coarse sea salt

1 cup chopped pecans, toasted (see sidebar, page 119)

WHEN COOKING SOAKED MILLET, *if you stir it often while simmering and slightly overcook it, the seeds will burst and release starch, creating a creamy consistency that's ideal for breakfast porridge. The addition of baked sweet potato, almond milk, and pureed cashews adds silky richness. Pecans provide depth and texture. Because whole grains are digested slowly, releasing their sugars into the bloodstream gradually, eating a hearty bowl of porridge in the morning will give you sustained energy and tide you over until lunch. Millet is high in vitamin B₆, niacin, and folic acid and also has significant amounts of magnesium, zinc, iron, calcium, and potassium. Note that if you make almond milk for this recipe, you should omit the sweetener.*

Preheat the oven to 400°F. With a fork, pierce the sweet potato in about 10 different places. Wrap it in aluminum foil and bake for 45 to 60 minutes, until fork-tender.

Meanwhile, toast the millet in a small saucepan over medium-high heat, stirring often with a wooden spoon, until the millet starts to smell nutty, about 3 minutes. Add the water and cinnamon stick. Increase the heat to high and bring to a boil. Immediately decrease the heat to low, cover, and simmer until all of the liquid is absorbed, about 30 minutes. Remove from the heat and let sit, covered, for about 10 minutes.

When the sweet potato is cool enough to handle, split it down the middle and scoop the flesh into a medium bowl. (Compost the skin.) Mash the sweet potato a bit, then add the almond milk, cashew cream, molasses, maple syrup, and salt and whisk until well blended. Add to the saucepan with the millet and mix well.

Bring to a boil over medium-high heat. Immediately decrease the heat to low and simmer, stirring frequently, until the porridge has thickened, about 10 minutes. Serve garnished with the pecans, drizzled with maple syrup, and finished with a splash of almond milk.

SWEET POTATO GRANOLA
with MOLASSES-GLAZED WALNUTS

OATS, SWEET POTATO, MAPLE SYRUP, SUNFLOWER OIL

YIELD 10 to 12 servings

SOUNDTRACK "The Bravest Man in the Universe" by Bobby Womack from *The Bravest Man in the Universe*

1 medium sweet potato (about 12 ounces)

3 cups old-fashioned rolled oats

½ cup maple syrup

½ cup sunflower oil

2 tablespoons maple sugar or date sugar

1 teaspoon unsulfured molasses

2 cups chopped Molasses-Glazed Walnuts (page 120)

1 teaspoon ground cinnamon

¼ teaspoon ground nutmeg

¼ teaspoon fine sea salt

I SELDOM PURCHASE GRANOLA. *I prefer to make it at home, coming up with my own recipes and sifting through cookbooks and online resources for interesting versions to try. This version pairs nicely with coconut milk yogurt and fresh fruit for a nutrient-packed breakfast. Rolled oats are a great source of fiber and high in folate, which is essential to a number of body functions. Walnuts are a rich source of omega-3 fatty acids; maple syrup contains calcium, potassium, iron, and magnesium.*

Preheat the oven to 400°F. With a fork, pierce the sweet potato in about 10 different places. Wrap it in aluminum foil and bake for 45 to 60 minutes, until fork-tender. Turn the oven down to 350°F.

When the sweet potato is cool enough to handle, split it down the middle and scoop the flesh into a bowl. Measure out 1 cup and reserve any remaining puree for another use.

Evenly spread the oats on a large, rimmed baking sheet and bake, stirring after 5 minutes for even toasting, for 10 minutes, until lightly toasted. Remove from the oven and turn the oven down to 300°F.

Meanwhile, put the maple syrup, oil, sugar, and molasses in a small saucepan. Cook over medium heat, stirring often, until the sugar is dissolved and the mixture is hot. Transfer to a blender and add the sweet potato, cover the blender with its lid, cover the lid with a kitchen towel, and process until smooth.

Line a large, rimmed baking sheet with parchment paper.

Put the oats, walnuts, cinnamon, nutmeg, and salt in a large bowl and mix well. Pour in the sweet potato mixture and stir until all the ingredients are well combined and the oats and walnuts are evenly coated. Transfer the mixture to the lined baking sheet and spread in an even layer with a rubber spatula.

Bake for 35 minutes, then break up and stir the mixture with a fork. Return to the oven and bake for about 10 minutes, until well toasted. Turn off the oven, partially open the oven door, and leave the granola in for 10 more minutes. Transfer the baking sheet to a rack and let cool to room temperature. Stored in a tightly sealed container in the refrigerator, it will keep for 1 month.

CAKES. TREATS. FRUIT.

AS NOTED on the website congocookbook.com, "Arabs, Asians, Europeans, and Indians, who have lived in Africa for generations, have brought their own traditions of sweets and desserts, which are well-known in many African countries." But from all available evidence, desserts are not part of the traditional African diet outside the northern regions of the continent. Customarily, Africans might have eaten fresh fruit or fruit salad after a meal, but nowadays creative desserts are cropping up throughout the continent.

Caribbean countries, on the other hand, have a rich history of tantalizing desserts inspired by culinary traditions of past European colonizers, the once-thriving sugarcane industry, and the abundance of a variety of flavorful tropical fruits. Of course, it's no secret that the Southern sweet tooth has led to the creation of some soul-satisfying desserts that have become favorites throughout the country, from puddings to layer cakes.

In this chapter, I offer an array of sweet things inspired by all these cultures, including a fresh fruit salad of pineapples, bananas, and mangoes tossed in a creamy mango-lime dressing; cold ice pops comprised of elements found in the classic Southern fruit salad ambrosia; a Bundt cake filled with nuts and fruit, dedicated to the grand dame of Southern cooking, Edna Lewis; and a bourbon-spiked vegan ice shake.

I'd be lying if I said I never eat things like cake, cookies, and ice cream for dessert after a home-cooked meal. If they're around, I'll eat them—usually too many of them. But at home I genuinely prefer to eat fresh, seasonal fruit to satisfy any cravings for something sweet after dinner. When I eat heavier sweets, I prefer them in the afternoon, so I have plenty of time to work off the extra calories. I never use white sugar, and I try to minimize my use of all-purpose flour, but I also don't let any drive to make desserts "healthy" compromise their flavor. The way I see it, maintaining a healthful diet provides some leeway to enjoy the occasional decadent dessert without any guilt.

AMBROSIA ICE POPS

ORANGE JUICE, ORANGE BLOSSOM WATER, COCONUT MILK, COCONUT YOGURT, COCONUT LIQUEUR

YIELD	SOUNDTRACK "Sir Greendown" by Janelle Monáe from *The ArchAndroid*
6 pops	

1¾ cups strained freshly squeezed navel orange juice

2 overly ripe bananas

2 teaspoons orange blossom water

¼ cup water

¼ cup raw cane sugar

2 tablespoons freshly squeezed Ruby Red grapefruit juice

½ teaspoon finely grated Ruby Red grapefruit zest

¾ cup coconut milk

½ cup plain coconut milk yogurt

2 teaspoons coconut liqueur

FRESH, FRUITY, CREAMY, *and sweet all in one frosty treat, these adult ice pops take their cue from ambrosia, a traditional fruit salad popular in the South that appeared in Southern cookbooks as early as the nineteenth century. Purists argue that ambrosia shouldn't include more than four ingredients: oranges, coconut, orange juice, and sugar. Other folks add an array of ingredients, including pineapple, mandarin oranges, various other fruits, nuts, marshmallows, and even creamy ingredients. The ingredients in these ice pops fall somewhere between minimal and over the top. Note that you'll need six ice-pop molds for this recipe. Big up to my assistant, Amanda Yee, for adding her magic to my original concept for this pop and making it stellar!*

Put the orange juice, bananas, and orange blossom water in a blender and process until smooth. Pour into 6 ice-pop molds, distributing it evenly among them. Each should be a little less than two-thirds full. Freeze until firm, about 2 hours.

Meanwhile, put the water, sugar, grapefruit juice, and grapefruit zest in a medium saucepan. Cook over medium-high heat, whisking constantly, until the sugar dissolves and the mixture thickens and forms a syrup, about 1 minute. Let cool completely.

Put the coconut milk, yogurt, and liqueur in a medium bowl. Slowly pour in the reserved grapefruit syrup, whisking constantly until smooth. Let cool briefly, then cover and refrigerate.

When the ice pops are firmly frozen, remove them from the freezer and top off each mold with the coconut milk mixture, leaving ¼ inch of space at the top to allow for expansion. Put the handle in each mold. Freeze until completely frozen, at least 6 hours or overnight.

To unmold, gently squeeze the pop as you pull the handle. If it doesn't release, run the molds under warm water for a few seconds and then try again.

COCONUT RICE PUDDING with NECTARINES

BASMATI RICE, COCONUT MILK, NECTARINES, PEACHES, LEMON JUICE, LEMON ZEST

YIELD	SOUNDTRACK "Freedom Highway" by The Staple Singers from *Freedom Highway*
4 servings	

2½ cups plus
  1 tablespoon water

¼ cup plus 1 teaspoon
  raw cane sugar

¼ teaspoon plus a pinch
  of coarse sea salt

½ vanilla bean

½ cup white basmati
  rice, soaked in water
  overnight and drained
  well

1 cup coconut milk, plus
  more for drizzling

¼ cup Creamed Cashews
  (page 143)

1½ cups peeled and
  finely diced nectarines
  (about 5 nectarines)

½ cup peeled and finely
  diced peaches (about
  2 peaches)

2 teaspoons freshly
  squeezed lemon juice

½ teaspoon finely grated
  lemon zest

Pinch of ground
  cinnamon

Black sesame seeds, for
  garnish

IN THE HEADNOTE *of her recipe for gossi, a Senegalese dish of rice cooked in milk, in* The Africa Cookbook, *Jessica B. Harris illuminates the thread of milk and rice dishes that pop up in different parts of the black world: "It is one of the links in the long chain that stretches from the gossi of Senegal through the arroz de viuva or milk rice of northeastern Brazil, to the rice desserts of the Caribbean, right into the rice pudding and milk rices of the American South." This version—a nod to Ghana, Georgia, and my good friend Kalalea, who lives in Salvador, Bahia—is simple and delicious. The combination of coconut milk and pureed cashews gives the pudding a thick, creamy, and satisfying mouthfeel, and the layers of nectarines in a peach puree make it refreshing and naturally sweet.*

Put 2½ cups of the water, ¼ cup of the sugar, and ¼ teaspoon of the salt in a medium saucepan. Cut the vanilla bean in half lengthwise. Scrape the seeds into the saucepan, then throw in the pod. Cook over medium-high heat, stirring constantly, until the sugar is dissolved and the mixture is boiling. Stir in the rice and return to a boil. Immediately decrease the heat to medium-low and simmer uncovered for 15 minutes, stirring often. Stir in the coconut milk and cashew cream and continue simmering, stirring often, until the texture is thick, like a porridge, about 15 minutes. Let cool completely.

Meanwhile, put the nectarines in a medium bowl. Put the peaches, lemon juice, lemon zest, cinnamon, and the remaining 1 tablespoon water, 1 teaspoon sugar, and pinch of salt in a blender and process until smooth. Pour over the nectarines and toss gently to combine. Cover and refrigerate until the rice has cooled.

To assemble each serving, spoon 3 tablespoons of the rice pudding into a ½-pint canning jar or other serving dish. Top with 3 tablespoons of the nectarines, then repeat the layers. Refrigerate until chilled, about 2 hours. Garnish with a sprinkling of black sesame seeds and a drizzle of coconut milk just before serving.

FIG and PEAR PASTELS

VANILLA BEAN, CINNAMON, LEMON JUICE, LEMON ZEST

YIELD about 7 servings (3 per person)

SOUNDTRACK "When I Lay My Burden Down" by Fred McDowell from *When I Lay My Burden Down*

FILLING
- 1 cup finely chopped dried figs
- 12 ounces Bosc or Asian pears, peeled and finely diced
- ¾ cup apple juice
- 1 tablespoon arrowroot powder
- ½ teaspoon ground cinnamon
- ⅛ teaspoon ground nutmeg
- ⅛ teaspoon fine sea salt
- 3 tablespoons agave nectar
- 3 tablespoons freshly squeezed lemon juice
- Finely grated zest of 1 lemon

DOUGH
- 1 tablespoon finely ground golden flaxseeds
- 6 tablespoons water
- 1¾ cups unbleached all-purpose flour

Coconut oil, for deep-frying (about 4 cups)

I'VE ALWAYS *wanted to create a dish that pays homage to the fried pies that my maternal grandmother made when I was a child. She filled them with peaches, figs, blackberries, pickled pears, and other fruits grown in her South Memphis neighborhood. They were slammin'! Rather than replicating Ma' Dear's hand pies, I make tiny baked turnovers inspired by pastels, a savory snack popular in Senegal. When I used to devour veggie pastels at Joloff, my neighborhood Senegalese restaurant in Brooklyn, I always wondered how they would taste filled with fruit. I modified a recipe for pastel pastry created by John O'Connor for the May 2012 issue of* Saveur. *These tasty treats bring South Memphis and Senegal together in delectable bites.*

To make the filling, put the figs in a medium heatproof bowl and add boiling water to cover. Let soak for about 10 minutes. Meanwhile, put the pears in a medium saucepan. In a small bowl, combine 3 tablespoons of the apple juice and the arrowroot powder, cinnamon, nutmeg, and salt and mix well until the arrowroot and spices are thoroughly blended. Transfer to the saucepan with the pears. Add the agave nectar, lemon juice, lemon zest, and the remaining apple juice. Drain the figs and add them to the saucepan. Cook the mixture over medium heat, stirring occasionally, until it begins to thicken, about 30 minutes. Remove from the heat and set aside to allow the mixture to cool and the flavors to deepen.

To make the dough, combine the flaxseeds and 3 tablespoons of the water in a medium bowl and stir with a fork until well mixed. Add the remaining 3 tablespoons water and the flour and stir until the mixture begins to form into a mass. Transfer to a lightly floured work surface. With clean hands, knead until the dough is smooth, about 5 minutes. Squeeze the dough into a tight ball. Flatten into a disk, wrap in plastic wrap, and let sit at room temperature for 1 hour.

With a rolling pin, roll out the dough until it is about ⅛ inch thick. Using a 3-inch round cutter, cut out about 21 circles from the dough. Place 1 super-heaping teaspoon of the fig and pear filling onto the center of one side of each circle. Fold the other half over to make a half-moon, press the edges to seal, then use the tines of a fork to make ridges around the sealed edge.

Warm 3 to 4 inches of the coconut oil in a small saucepan over medium-high heat until hot but not smoking, about 350°F. Working in batches, fry the pies until golden, about 5 minutes. Serve hot.

COCOA-SPICE CAKE with CRYSTALLIZED GINGER and COCONUT-CHOCOLATE GANACHE

NUTMEG, CAYENNE, COCONUT MILK, AVOCADO, JAMAICAN RUM, CRYSTALLIZED GINGER

YIELD 8 to 16 servings	**SOUNDTRACK** "Marcus Garvey" by Burning Spear from *Marcus Garvey/Garvey's Ghost*	**BOOK** *The Other Side of Paradise: A Memoir* by Staceyann Chin

CAKE

- ¼ cup coconut oil, melted, plus more for oiling
- 1 cup plus 1 tablespoon fine raw cane sugar
- ¾ cup whole wheat pastry flour
- ¾ cup unbleached all-purpose flour
- 6 tablespoons unsweetened natural cocoa powder (not Dutch-processed)
- 1¼ teaspoons baking soda
- ½ teaspoon fine sea salt
- Scant ½ teaspoon cayenne pepper
- ¼ teaspoon ground nutmeg
- ½ cup plus 2 tablespoons coconut milk
- ¼ cup packed mashed ripe avocado (about ½ medium avocado)
- 2 tablespoons plus 1 teaspoon dark Jamaican rum
- 1 tablespoon apple cider vinegar
- 1 teaspoon vanilla extract
- 3 ounces crystallized ginger, finely chopped (about ½ cup)

GANACHE

- 5 ounces unsweetened baking chocolate, finely chopped
- ¾ cup coconut milk
- 5 tablespoons raw cane sugar
- ⅛ teaspoon cayenne pepper
- 1 tablespoon dark Jamaican rum (optional)

- 12 thin slices crystallized ginger

WHENEVER I SERVE THIS CAKE, *folks can't believe it's vegan, and they always get a kick out of it when I tell them that I include avocado to add moisture and natural creaminess. My assistant, Amanda Yee, came up with the idea of pouring a coconut-chocolate ganache over the cake. You can stop there and enjoy chocolaty bliss, or take it to the next level by pairing it with Vanilla Spice Rum Shakes (opposite). (Pictured on page 172.)*

To make the cake, preheat the oven to 375°F. Oil an 8-inch round cake pan with 2-inch sides.

Sift the sugar, flours, cocoa powder, baking soda, salt, cayenne, and nutmeg into a large bowl and stir with a whisk until well blended.

Put the coconut milk, oil, avocado, rum, vinegar, and vanilla extract in a blender and process until smooth (or put them in a large bowl and blend with an immersion blender until smooth). Make a well in the center of the dry ingredients and add the wet ingredients and the ginger.

Fold together until uniformly mixed. Scrape the batter into the prepared pan and spread in an even layer. Bake for 30 to 40 minutes, until a toothpick inserted in the center comes out clean. Let cool in the pan for 15 minutes. Slide a butter knife around the edge, then invert the cake onto a rack and let cool to room temperature.

To make the ganache, put the chocolate in a medium heatproof bowl. Put the coconut milk, sugar, and cayenne in a small saucepan and heat until steaming hot (avoid boiling), stirring often, until the sugar has dissolved. Slowly pour over the chocolate and let stand until the chocolate is melted, 3 to 5 minutes. Add the rum and whisk until completely smooth. Let stand at room temperature, stirring occasionally, until slightly cooled but pourable, about 5 minutes.

To glaze the cake, pour the ganache evenly over the cake and let stand until the ganache is set, about 30 minutes. Garnish with the ginger slices.

VANILLA SPICE ICE CREAM

NUTMEG, VANILLA BEAN, RAW CANE SUGAR, COCONUT MILK, CASHEWS

YIELD 4 to 6 servings | **SOUNDTRACK** "Á La Mode" by Art Blakey & The Jazz Messengers from *Jazz Messengers*

½ cup cooked navy or cannellini beans, drained

2 cups coconut milk

½ cup plus 2 tablespoons raw cane sugar

1 teaspoon unsulfured molasses

⅛ teaspoon ground cinnamon

⅛ teaspoon freshly ground nutmeg

¼ teaspoon allspice berries, toasted (see sidebar, page 9) and ground

⅛ teaspoon fine sea salt

1 vanilla bean

½ cup Cashew Cream (see page 143)

MY BUDDY MATT HALTEMAN *suggested that I use white beans in this ice cream to give it a creamier consistency. Although I typically recommend cooking beans from scratch, using canned is fine for this recipe; just rinse them well before blending. When I was making final edits to this book, someone gifted me with a copy of Smoke and Pickles, by chef Edward Lee. He includes a recipe for Cornbread-Sorghum Milkshake, which inspired me to create the unbelievably creamy Vanilla Spice Bourbon/Rum Shake, described in the sidebar.*

Allspice is one of the most important ingredients in Caribbean cuisine, and it makes this ice cream a delicious and appropriate accompaniment for Cocoa-Spice Cake with Crystallized Ginger and Coconut-Chocolate Ganache (page 174). Feel free to modify the basic recipe to come up with your own versions. Change the spices or add fresh fruit and make it your own.

Put the beans and coconut milk in a blender and process until creamy. Strain through a fine-mesh sieve into a medium saucepan. Stir in the sugar, molasses, cinnamon, nutmeg, allspice, and salt. Cut the vanilla bean in half lengthwise. Scrape the seeds into the saucepan, then throw in the pod. Cook over medium heat, whisking occasionally, until the sugar has dissolved and the mixture is gently simmering, 3 to 5 minutes. Stir in the cashew cream.

Remove from the heat and let cool completely. Transfer to a medium bowl, cover, and refrigerate until completely chilled, about 6 hours or overnight.

Remove the vanilla pod, pour the mixture into an ice cream maker, and freeze according to the manufacturer's instructions. Transfer to an airtight container and freeze until firm, about 8 hours or overnight.

VANILLA SPICE BOURBON/RUM SHAKE

To make one serving, put ½ cup Vanilla Spice Ice Cream in a blender. Add ¼ cup Date-Sweetened Almond Milk (page 152) and 1 tablespoon of bourbon or rum (or to taste) and pulse until thick and creamy. (Pictured on page 172.)

SPICED PERSIMMON BUNDT CAKE
with ORANGE GLAZE

HACHIYA PERSIMMON, CINNAMON, NUTMEG, CLOVES

YIELD 8 to 16 servings || **SOUNDTRACK** "A Piece of Ground" by Miriam Makeba, from *Miriam Makeba in Concert* || **BOOK** *To Us, All Flowers Are Roses: Poems* by Lorna Goodison

CAKE

- 1 cup coconut oil, plus more for oiling
- 1 cup whole wheat pastry flour
- 2 cups unbleached all-purpose flour
- 2 teaspoons baking soda
- 2 teaspoons baking powder
- 2 teaspoons ground cinnamon
- 1 teaspoon fine sea salt
- ½ teaspoon ground nutmeg
- ¼ teaspoon ground cloves
- 2 heaping tablespoons finely ground golden flaxseeds
- 6 tablespoons water
- 2 cups raw cane sugar
- 2 cups persimmon puree (3 to 5 large hachiya persimmons)
- 2 tablespoons apple cider vinegar
- 2 cups walnuts, toasted and skinned (see sidebar), then chopped

IN 2012 *I became acquainted with photographer John T. Hill, an old friend of Edna Lewis who frequently collaborated with her. He sent me a copy of the summer 2012 issue of Edible Blue Ridge, which featured an article about Miss Lewis that included a photograph that he took of her for Vogue (see page 178). At the time, I had no idea what kind of cake she had made for the photo, and I imagined that it was a persimmon cake. A passage from The Taste of Country Cooking in which Edna Lewis describes "finding walnuts [and] picking persimmons" in Freetown, Virginia (her birthplace), undoubtedly colored my vision of the cake in the photo. I later discovered that it was a Christmas fruitcake, but I decided to run with my imagined version of the dessert. (Pictured on page 179.) While this cake is meant to showcase the flavor of hachiya persimmons, you can substitute more applesauce for the persimmon puree if they are out of season or unavailable. The cake is delicious as is, but to take it over the top, serve it with Sweet Orange Blossom Cream (page 146) or Vanilla Spice Ice Cream (page 175). Here's to the grande dame of Southern cooking, Miss Edna Lewis. Note: to make persimmon puree, simply peel the persimmons and puree in a blender.*

To make the cake, preheat the oven to 350°F. Oil a 10-inch Bundt pan.

Sift the flours, baking soda, baking powder, cinnamon, salt, nutmeg, and cloves into a large bowl and stir with a whisk until well blended.

In the bowl of a stand mixer or in a medium bowl with a handheld mixer, combine the flaxseeds and water and beat on high speed until well blended, about 30 seconds. Add the oil and sugar and beat on high speed for about 3 minutes. Add the persimmon puree and vinegar and beat on high speed for about 3 minutes. Immediately add to the flour mixture and stir just until combined. Fold in the walnuts.

Pour the batter into the prepared pan and spread in an even layer. Bake for about 45 minutes, until a toothpick inserted into the center comes out clean. Let cool for 15 minutes, then turn out onto a rack to cool completely.

GLAZE

2 cups confectioners' sugar, sifted

2 tablespoons freshly squeezed orange juice

2 tablespoons freshly squeezed lemon juice

1 teaspoon finely grated lemon zest

To make the glaze, put the sugar, orange juice, lemon juice, and lemon zest in a medium bowl and stir until smooth.

To glaze the cake, pour the glaze evenly over the cake in a thin layer and let stand until the glaze is set, about 15 minutes.

TOASTING WALNUTS AND REMOVING THEIR SKINS

While naturally sweet in flavor, walnuts have a bitter outer skin. To remove the skin, first preheat the oven to 350°F. Spread the walnuts on a parchment paper–lined baking sheet and toast for 8 minutes, stirring halfway through. Remove from the oven and set aside until the walnuts are cool enough to touch. Transfer the walnuts to a sieve and, holding the sieve over the sink, rub the walnuts against the wire until the skins loosen and fall off. Set aside to completely cool.

Although you will get the freshest, most flavorful walnuts by purchasing them in the shell and cracking them just before using, this process can be time-consuming. So I buy shelled walnut halves and store them in the freezer to extend their freshness.

TROPICAL FRUIT SALAD
with MANGO-LIME DRESSING

MANGO, PINEAPPLE, BANANA, GINGER, LIME ZEST, LIME JUICE, MINT

YIELD 4 to 6 servings | **SOUNDTRACK** "Good Vibes / Dub Vibes" by Horace Andy from *Good Vibes* | **BOOK** *Riddym Ravings and Other Poems* by Jean "Binta" Breeze

2½ cups diced ripe but firm mangoes (3 to 4 mangoes)

3 tablespoon freshly squeezed lime juice

1 teaspoon agave nectar, or to taste

Pinch of coarse sea salt

3 cups chopped pineapple, in ½-inch chunks (about 1 pineapple)

2 bananas, sliced ½ inch thick

1 tablespoon finely grated lime zest

1 teaspoon minced fresh ginger

1 tablespoon minced fresh mint

MY FAVORITE *sweet after a meal is a piece of fresh, seasonal, and perfectly ripe fruit. I prefer eating fruit from local farmers' markets, but sometimes I indulge in imported tropical fruit. As far as fruit salads go, this one is simply delicious. Fresh mango, pineapple, and banana tossed in a creamy sweet-and-tangy mango-lime dressing make this juicy dish irresistible. Seriously, I always try to make this salad last for a few days, but before the night is over, it's gone.*

Since most mangoes and pineapples are imported, you can get them throughout the year, but be sure to use fruit at the peak of its flavor. Pineapples stop ripening once they're harvested. For optimum flavor, choose a pineapple that has a fragrant, sweet smell at the stem end—and that doesn't smell fermented. Mangoes should be soft to the touch and have a fruity aroma at their stem end.

Put ½ cup of the diced mangoes in a blender. Add the lime juice, agave nectar, and salt and blend until creamy.

Put the pineapple, bananas, lime zest, ginger, and the remaining 2 cups mangoes in a medium bowl and stir gently to combine. Pour the dressing over the salad and toss gently to combine. Cover and refrigerate until chilled, about 1 hour.

Just before serving, add the mint and toss gently to combine. Serve in chilled bowls.

DATE, NUT, and CRANBERRY BALLS

PECANS, ALMONDS, CINNAMON, GINGER

YIELD about 12 servings (1 ball per serving)

SOUNDTRACK "Higher" by Oh No from *Dr. No's Oxperiment*

1 cup pitted Medjool dates

1 cup raw almonds

½ cup raw pecans

¼ teaspoon ground cinnamon

⅛ teaspoon ground ginger

⅛ teaspoon fine sea salt

1 cup unsweetened dried cranberries

THIS RECIPE *is inspired by three dishes: kashata, a popular East African snack made with various combinations of spices, peanuts, and grated coconut; a recipe for coconut-almond balls with dried fruit featured in Ani's Raw Food Essentials, by my good friend cookbook author Ani Phyo; and Moroccan majoun, a cannabis-filled snack famous for its aphrodisiac qualities.*

If you're an adult resident of Colorado or Washington State, feel free to honor the spirit of traditional majoun. Combine 1 cup coconut oil with ¼ ounce finely ground high-quality dried cannabis buds in a small skillet over low heat and simmer for about 30 minutes. Strain the coconut oil and add a few teaspoons of it to the food processor along with the dates, saving the remaining oil for another use.

Put the dates in a small heatproof bowl and add boiling water to cover. Cover and let soak for 5 minutes. Drain well.

In a food processor fitted with the metal blade, combine the almonds, pecans, cinnamon, ginger, and salt and pulse until very finely ground. Add the dates and process until the mixture is a well-blended sticky mass. Transfer to a medium bowl, add the cranberries, and thoroughly mix with your hands. Clean your hands but leave them a little wet. Roll the mixture into 1-inch balls (about the size of walnuts) between your palms. You may need to remoisten your hands about halfway through if they get too sticky. Enjoy immediately, or store in an airtight container in a cool, dark place for up to 1 month.

COLD DRINKS. TONICS. COCKTAILS.

BY NOW, most of us are aware that sugary drinks are a major contributor to a number of easily preventable diet-related health conditions. It is recommended that adults have no more than two tablespoons of sugar per day in order to maintain a healthful diet, and the average American adult has well above that. Get this: it is estimated that American children (between the ages of four and eight years old) are consuming an average of seven tablespoons of sugar per day, and a number of those calories come from sugary drinks (aka liquid candy). While "fruit" juices with lots of added sugar are a contributing factor, the majority of extra calories come from sodas, which U.S. beverage companies spend around $3 billion per year marketing to us.

I drink lots of water, fruit smoothies, herbal teas, and freshly pressed vegetable juices throughout the day. Don't get me wrong, I enjoy sugary drinks. I simply treat them and alcoholic beverages (which contain a lot of sugar) the same way I treat dessert: I have them on special occasions. Starting with my first book, *Grub*, I've taken pleasure in creating diverse beverages for such moments: refreshing cold drinks inspired by seasonal ingredients, soothing toddies that warm from the inside out, and festive cocktails dedicated to people who inspire me. This chapter, which includes everything from kid-friendly fruit-filled drinks to crunk cocktails for the grown and sexy, has recipes for every season.

Serve Gunpowder Lemonade (page 194) to celebrate spring's bounty. Pour the kids Grape-Tarragon Spritzer (page 193) at summer cookouts while the old folks enjoy cocktails like the mango-and-ginger-based Amy Ashwood (page 186) and the watermelon-based Red Summer (page 195). In the fall, everyone will sip Roselle-Rooibos Drink (page 191) and Tamarind Sweet Tea (page 196) with relish, and over the holiday—when the kids are asleep—the Congo Square (page 189) and Black Queen (page 188) will promote lively conversations, dancing, and frolicking.

SIMPLE SYRUP

RAW CANE SUGAR

YIELD
1 cup

SOUNDTRACK "Wild" by J Dilla from *Ruff Draft* (2007 Reissue)

1 cup raw cane sugar
½ cup water

I AM VERY CLEAR that a lot of people who buy this book need to try to limit the amount of sugar that they consume, if not avoid it all together. There is a sizable body of research about the negative impacts of excessive sugar consumption, and I often discuss the need to curb sugar intake for optimal health and well-being. I also believe that a sweet drink every now and then will not have a negative impact on our overall well-being if it's in the context of a healthful diet. I'm guessing many of you feel the same way.

The drinks in this chapter were created in the spirit of fun and refreshing beverages that you might have at a party, enjoy at a restaurant, or relax with on the weekend. Here, I offer a basic simple syrup recipe, and I provide instructions to make flavored syrups for the Strawberry-Watermelon Salad (page 39) earlier in this book and the drink recipes in this chapter. If you have any leftover simple syrup, it will last a long time refrigerated. I try to use flavored syrups within two weeks, however. Of course, you could always substitute agave nectar for the raw cane sugar called for in these recipes. I just find that the latter has a cleaner taste and does not get in the way of the other ingredients.

Combine the sugar and the water in a small saucepan over low heat. Stir well. Heat until hot to the touch and the sugar is completely dissolved, about 3 minutes. Let cool and refrigerate until ready to use.

FLAVORED SIMPLE SYRUPS

BASIL-CAYENNE

Prepare the simple syrup as directed above, adding 1 teaspoon cayenne pepper and $^1/_4$ cup packed minced fresh basil before bringing the mixture to a boil. Remove from the heat and let steep for 8 hours or overnight. Strain through a fine-mesh sieve into a glass jar and refrigerate until ready to use. (Compost the basil.)

VANILLA BEAN

Split 2 vanilla beans in half and scrape out their seeds. Prepare the simple syrup as directed above, adding the vanilla beans and their seeds before bringing the mixture to a boil. Remove from the heat and let steep for 8 hours or overnight. Strain through a fine-mesh sieve into a glass jar and refrigerate until ready to use.

LEMON-TARRAGON

Prepare the simple syrup as directed, adding the finely grated zest of 1 lemon and $^1/_4$ cup packed minced fresh tarragon before bringing the mixture to a boil. Remove from the heat and let steep for 8 hours or overnight. Strain through a fine-mesh sieve into a glass jar and refrigerate until ready to use. (Compost the tarragon.)

SPEARMINT

Prepare the simple syrup as directed, adding $^1/_2$ cup packed minced fresh spearmint before bringing the mixture to a boil. Remove from the heat and let steep for 8 hours or overnight. Strain through a fine-mesh sieve into a glass jar until ready to use. (Compost the mint.)

BASIL-HABANERO

Prepare the simple syrup as directed, adding $^1/_2$ teaspoon minced habanero chile with seeds and $^1/_4$ cup packed minced fresh basil before bringing the mixture to a boil. Remove from the heat and let steep for 8 hours or overnight. Strain through a fine-mesh sieve into a glass jar and refrigerate until ready to use. (Compost the habanero and basil.)

AMY ASHWOOD

GINGER, MANGO, VODKA, LIME JUICE, CAYENNE

YIELD
2 servings

SOUNDTRACK "Africa Unite" by Bob Marley and the Wailers from *Survival*

Ice, for shaking the cocktail

6 fluid ounces Mango Nectar (see sidebar, page 188)

½ teaspoon fresh ginger juice

1 fluid ounce freshly squeezed lime juice

3 fluid ounces vodka

2 thin slices crystallized ginger

Cayenne pepper, for garnish

WHILE THERE ARE A NUMBER *of streets, parks, and libraries across the globe dedicated to the late Pan-Africanist Marcus Garvey, very little has been created to honor the memory of his first wife, Amy Ashwood Garvey. As explained by professor Frederick Douglass Opie in a series of online videos, Amy Ashwood was a cofounder of the Universal Negro Improvement Association (UNIA) with Garvey, and she played a central role in founding a number of UNIA restaurants in Harlem. She also opened the Florence Mills Restaurant and Social Club in London, which served Caribbean food. It also functioned as a gathering spot for African and Afro-Caribbean student activists and played a crucial role in the growth of Pan-African politics in the United Kingdom.*

In a nod to Ashwood's Jamaican heritage, this cocktail features classic Caribbean flavors and ingredients—tropical fruit (mango and lime), spice (ginger), and heat (cayenne). The mango and ginger base pairs nicely with vodka and makes this a refreshing drink to enjoy on a hot summer day, and the crystallized ginger absolutely gilds the lily.

Fill a cocktail shaker with ice and add the nectar, ginger juice, lime juice, and vodka. Shake well, then strain evenly into 2 glasses. Garnish each serving with the crystallized ginger and a small pinch of cayenne pepper.

JUICING GINGER

The easiest way to get ginger juice is to feed fresh ginger root into an electric juicer. If you don't have a juicer, coarsely grate ginger knobs (no need to peel them) or pulverize them in a food processor, then wrap the pulp in cheesecloth and squeeze to extract all the juice. You can also squeeze the pulp with your hands, then strain the juice.

{ continued }

MANGO NECTAR

YIELD about 2½ cups, or enough to make about 6 cocktails

3½ cups water
½ cup raw cane sugar
1 cup diced very ripe mango (about 1 large mango)

This nectar was made for the Amy Ashwood, but you could also enjoy it as a nonalcoholic quaff by doctoring it up with a bit of freshly squeezed lime juice and adding sparkling water.

Put the water, sugar, and mango in a blender and puree until smooth. Transfer to a small saucepan and bring to a simmer over medium-high heat. Decrease the heat to medium-low and simmer, stirring occasionally, until the liquid is reduced to about 2½ cups, about 10 minutes. Let cool for 1 hour.

Transfer to a jar, seal tightly, and refrigerate until chilled, about 3 hours. Stored in the refrigerator, it will keep for about 7 days.

BLACK QUEEN

ORANGE PEKOE TEA, LEMON JUICE, SPARKLING WINE

YIELD 8 servings	**SOUNDTRACK** "Odun De! Odun De! (Aw Dun Day! Aw Dun Day!)" by Babatunde Olatunji from *Drums of Passion*	**BOOK** *Harlem Nocturne: Women Artists and Progressive Politics During World War II* by Farah Jasmine Griffin

2¾ cups water
6 orange pekoe tea bags
2½ fluid ounces simple syrup (page 184)
1 fluid ounce freshly squeezed lemon juice
1 (750 ml) bottle sparkling white wine, chilled

I THINK OF this drink as the older, elegant auntie of Southern sweet iced tea. Inspired by mimosas, the Black Queen is a tea concentrate (you can make it well in advance) topped off with white sparkling wine. I imagine this drink providing a lively New Year's toast.

Put the water and tea bags in a small saucepan and bring to a boil over high heat. Immediately remove from the heat, cover, and let steep for 30 minutes.

Uncover and let cool to room temperature. Remove the tea bags with a slotted spoon, pressing them gently to extract as much liquid as possible. Stir in the simple syrup and lemon juice, then freeze just until ice begins to form. For each serving, pour 3 fluid ounces of the tea concentrate into a chilled champagne flute or wineglass and top off with 3 fluid ounces of the sparkling wine.

CONGO SQUARE

COCONUT MILK, CASHEWS, COCONUT WATER, DARK RUM, NUTMEG, CINNAMON

YIELD
2 servings

SOUNDTRACK "The Uprising" by Christian Scott from *Anthem*

BOOK *The World That Made New Orleans: From Spanish Silver to Congo Square* by Ned Sublette

FILM: *Toussaint L'Ouverture* directed by Philippe Niang

2 fluid ounces coconut milk

2 fluid ounces Creamed Cashews (see page 143)

2 fluid ounces coconut water

2 fluid ounces dark rum

2 pinches of finely grated lemon zest

¾ fluid ounce Vanilla Bean Syrup (see page 185)

2 large pinches of freshly ground nutmeg

2 small pinches of ground cinnamon

THIS RICH AND VELVETY cocktail is very satisfying to drink. I prefer it warm during the colder months, but it's also enjoyable cold or at room temperature during other times of the year. It is primarily inspired by two traditional holiday drinks: kremas, a Haitian drink made from creamed coconut, sweetened condensed milk, and rum; and milk punch, a sweetened milk and bourbon concoction popular in New Orleans and other parts of the South. I created this cocktail to symbolize the shared history and interconnection of New Orleans and Haiti that dates back to the eighteenth century.

To this day, if you look with a careful eye, you can see the influence of Haiti throughout New Orleans, from the architecture to the cuisine. New Orleans, which had the largest antebellum slave market in the nation, received a huge influx of Haitians (over ten thousand) during the Haitian Revolution (1791–1803). I imagine that many of the newly arrived Africans from Haiti built community with other Africans at Congo Square, a space where Africans came from miles around to gather on Sundays, playing drums, dancing, and preserving traditions.

Put the coconut milk, cashew cream, coconut water, rum, lemon zest, and vanilla syrup in a small saucepan. Cook over medium heat, stirring often, until warmed though and thoroughly combined, about 3 minutes. Divide evenly into 2½-pint Mason jars or mugs. Garnish each drink with the nutmeg and cinnamon and serve immediately.

ROSELLE-ROOIBOS DRINK

HIBISCUS, ROOIBOS TEA, ORANGE JUICE, CINNAMON, PINEAPPLE

YIELD 4 to 6 servings

SOUNDTRACK "Put Some Red on It" (Machinedrum Remix) by Spoek Mathambo from *Put Some Red on It*

BOOK *Gully* by Roger Bonair-Agard

6½ cups water

2 (2-inch) cinnamon sticks

6 tea bags or 3 tablespoons rooibos tea

2 cups dried hibiscus flowers

¾ cup freshly squeezed orange juice

1 cup agave nectar

2 cups cubed fresh pineapple, in 1-inch chunks, plus 6 spears

Ice, for serving

BOTH ROOIBOS AND ROSELLE have health-supportive properties. Rooibos is high in antioxidants and a number of minerals, including copper, iron, potassium, calcium, zinc, manganese, and magnesium. Healers in Africa, Asia, and Latin America have traditionally used roselle, a type of hibiscus, to treat a number of ailments. This drink is tart, sweet, and floral and has become one of my favorite summertime beverages. In this recipe, I call for fresh pineapple to give the drink texture and vibrant tropical flavor, but when my editor, Melissa Moore, brought me a bag of fresh peaches from the farm of Mas Masumoto, I peeled, sliced, and used them in place of the pineapple. It was off the chain! I think any other stone fruit, such as nectarines or cherries, would also work well, and I encourage you to experiment with adding them. For a late fall or winter spin, serve this drink warm, omitting the fresh fruit and boiling the tea and hibiscus with ¼ teaspoon whole cloves, in a nod to how roselle is prepared in Trinidad and Tobago.

Put the water and cinnamon in a medium saucepan. Bring to a boil over high heat, then boil for 2 minutes. Add the rooibos, hibiscus flowers, orange juice, and agave nectar and mix well. Immediately remove from the heat, cover, and let stand for 30 minutes.

Uncover and let cool to room temperature. Strain through a fine-mesh sieve into a pitcher, pressing down on the solids to extract as much liquid as possible. (Compost the solids.) Add the pineapple chunks and refrigerate for at least 8 hours or overnight.

Serve over ice, garnishing each glass with a pineapple spear.

CUCUMBER-LEMON WATER

CUCUMBER, LEMON JUICE

YIELD 4 to 6 servings

SOUNDTRACK "So Fresh, So Clean (Blues Cover)" by Xiomara from *XXX*

1 English cucumber, peeled, halved crosswise, and quartered lengthwise

8 cups water

1 tablespoon freshly squeezed lemon juice

THIS IS NOT SO MUCH *a recipe as an attempt to encourage you to drink more water. Cucumbers contain vitamin A, potassium, magnesium, phosphorous, and manganese, and the lemon juice is alkalizing. Since many imbalances can occur in our bodies from over-acidity, ensuring that we have an acid-alkaline balance is important for optimal health.*

Put the cucumber in a large pitcher. Add the water and gently stir in the lemon juice.

Refrigerate until chilled, at least 1 hour. Stored in the refrigerator, it will keep for about 3 days.

GINGER-LEMONGRASS TONIC

GINGER, LEMONGRASS, LEMON JUICE, MAPLE SYRUP

YIELD about 4 servings

SOUNDTRACK "Juiced" by THEESatisfaction from *awE naturalE*

BOOK *Cereus Blooms at Night* by Shani Mootoo

6 tablespoons Grade B maple syrup

2 tablespoons freshly squeezed lemon juice

1 tablespoon apple cider vinegar

1 (3-inch) knob fresh ginger, peeled and sliced into paper-thin rounds

6 cups water

2 lemongrass stalks, ends trimmed and thinly sliced

I CREATED THIS DRINK *in the spirit of healing tonics that have been used in many cultures to support overall health and well-being. Inspired by citronelle, a traditional tea from the Ivory Coast, this tonic uses lemongrass, as well as fresh ginger. Both promote digestion and help provide relief from flatulence. It also contains apple cider vinegar, which helps alkalize the body and brings balance to overacidity. In a shout-out to the Master Cleanse, the addition of maple syrup makes this a satisfying drink for ending a savory meal on a sweet note. Sipping on 1 cup should be sufficient to aid in digestion.*

Put the maple syrup, lemon juice, and vinegar in a heatproof pitcher and mix well. Stir in the ginger. Put the water and lemongrass in a medium saucepan over high heat and bring to a boil. Immediately decrease the heat to medium-low, cover, and simmer for 30 minutes.

Pour the lemongrass infusion into the pitcher and let cool to room temperature. Cover and refrigerate for at least 8 hours. Strain through a fine-mesh sieve, pressing the solids to extract as much liquid as possible. (Compost the solids.) Serve chilled. Stored in the refrigerator, it will keep for 5 days.

GRAPE-TARRAGON SPRITZER

RED GRAPE JUICE, LEMON JUICE, LEMON ZEST, TARRAGON, SPARKLING WATER

YIELD 4 to 6 servings | **SOUNDTRACK** "Getting There" by Flying Lotus (featuring Niki Randa) from *Until Quiet Comes*

- 1½ pounds seedless red grapes (preferably organic), stemmed
- 3 tablespoons freshly squeezed lemon juice
- ¼ cup Lemon-Tarragon Syrup (page 185)
- 4 cups sparkling water, chilled until almost frozen
- Tarragon sprigs, for garnish

ACCORDING TO the Oxford Companion to Wine, *before 1952, Algerian, Moroccan, and Tunisian wine accounted for nearly two-thirds of the total international wine trade, so I felt compelled to create a grape-based drink in honor of that history. Grapes are full of vitamins K and C, and tarragon is a great source of niacin, phosphorous, and copper. The aniselike flavor of tarragon syrup and sweet grape juice go well together in this concoction. Topping off the concentrate with sparkling water and adding frozen grapes make this a refreshing, modern drink for a summer garden party. I could also see using the concentrate as the base for cooling ice pops—just add a bit more tarragon syrup, as freezing tends to make things taste less sweet.*

Put one-third of of the grapes on a large plate and freeze until completely frozen, at least 3 hours.

Put the remaining grapes in a blender and process until completely broken down. Strain through a fine-mesh sieve into a serving pitcher, pressing down on the solids to extract as much liquid as possible.

(Compost the solids.) This should yield about 1¼ cups juice. Add the lemon juice and tarragon syrup and mix well. Add the sparkling water and stir *gently* to combine.

To serve, put a handful of frozen grapes in each glass and garnish with a sprig of tarragon.

GUNPOWDER LEMONADE

GUNPOWDER GREEN TEA, LEMON JUICE, SPEARMINT

YIELD 4 to 6 servings ‖ **SOUNDTRACK** "El-Maddahine" by Chalf Hassan from *Bazaar Marrakesh* ‖ **FILM:** *Negroes with Guns: Rob Williams and Black Power* directed by Sandra Dickson and Churchill Roberts

9½ cups water

Scant ¼ cup gunpowder (pearl) green tea leaves or other Chinese green tea leaves

¾ cup freshly squeezed lemon juice

½ cup plus 2 tablespoons Spearmint Syrup (page 185)

Ice, for serving

Spearmint sprigs, for garnish

MINT TEA HOLDS A SPECIAL PLACE in *North Africa, where the ritualized nature of making and drinking it is an integral part of social and cultural life, similar to how making and serving coffee is in Ethiopia. The national drink of Morocco, it's consumed throughout the day and served to guests as a gesture of hospitality. Tea culture is also important to daily life in many parts of West Africa, and mint tea is enjoyed during midday breaks and after dinner. As Jessica B. Harris explains in* The Africa Cookbook, *the Senegalese make a unique version of mint tea; it has the same ingredients as Moroccan mint tea—Chinese gunpowder green tea and fresh mint—but it's prepared differently in a tea ceremony called attaya, in which tea is served in three rounds.*

Here I've combined Chinese gunpowder green tea with spearmint syrup and fresh lemon juice to make an invigorating, minty green tea lemonade. I use the traditional Chinese method of preparing green tea to ensure that the flavor isn't too bitter. Green tea has a high number of antioxidants, and studies have found that drinking it is associated with a reduced risk of heart disease and certain cancers, so enjoying it a few times per week is probably a good practice.

Put 2 cups of the water in a medium saucepan and bring to a boil over high heat. Let cool for 5 minutes. Add the tea and swirl around for 10 seconds to rinse the tea. Immediately drain the tea leaves in a fine-mesh sieve, discarding the liquid.

Put the remaining 7½ cups water in the same saucepan and bring to a boil over high heat. Let cool for 7 minutes. Add the tea leaves, swirl around for about 5 seconds, and cover. After 2 minutes, strain the tea through the fine-mesh sieve into a heatproof pitcher. (Compost the tea leaves.)

Add the lemon juice and Spearmint Syrup. Taste and add more syrup if desired. Let cool to room temperature, then refrigerate until chilled, about 3 hours. Serve in tall glasses over ice, garnished with a sprig of spearmint.

RED SUMMER

WATERMELON JUICE, VODKA, BASIL, HABANERO, CLUB SODA

YIELD
2 servings

SOUNDTRACK "Riot" by Herbie Hancock
from *Speak Like a Child*

BOOK *Red Summer: The Summer of 1919 and the
Awakening of Black America* by Cameron McWhirter

Ice, for shaking the
cocktail and for
serving

4 fluid ounces fresh red
watermelon juice (see
sidebar)

3 fluid ounces vodka

2 fluid ounce freshly
squeezed lemon juice

½ fluid ounce Basil-
Habanero Syrup
(see page 185)

4 fluid ounces chilled
club soda

2 wedges red watermelon
with rind, about
2 inches long and
½ inch thick

THIS IS A REMIX *of my Fresh Watermelon Vodka "Martini" from Vegan Soul
Kitchen. The combination of vodka with lime, orange, and watermelon juice made
that drink an intensely flavored aperitif. This drink goes in a different direction and
combines fragrant and spicy Basil-Habanero Syrup, fruity watermelon, crisp vodka,
and invigorating club soda, making it a refreshing cocktail to be enjoyed anytime of the
day. There's something about the clean flavor of vodka and fresh red watermelon juice
that just yells, screams, and hollers summer.*

Fill a cocktail shaker with ice and add
the watermelon juice, vodka, lemon juice,
and the Basil-Habanero Syrup. Shake well,
then strain evenly into 2 tall, slim glasses
filled with ice. Gently stir 2 ounces of club
soda into each glass and garnish with a
watermelon wedge.

MAKING WATERMELON JUICE

To make watermelon juice, cut watermelon off the rind into chunks.
Add the chunks to an upright blender, puree until liquefied, then
strain through a fine-mesh sieve to remove all solids. (Compost
the pulp.) Every 3 pounds of watermelon (with rind) usually yields
3½ to 4 cups of juice.

TAMARIND SWEET TEA

TAMARIND, ORANGE PEKOE TEA, ORANGE JUICE, VANILLA BEAN

YIELD 4 to 6 servings || **SOUNDTRACK** "Who's In Charge" by Silhouette Brown from *Silhouette Brown* | **BOOK** *For Women and the Nation: Funmilayo Ransome-Kuti of Nigeria* by Cheryl Johnson-Odim and Nina Emma Mba

1 pound fresh tamarind pods, 12 ounces tamarind pulp, or 1 cup tamarind paste

9½ cups water

6 orange pekoe tea bags

½ cup freshly squeezed orange juice

½ cup Vanilla Bean Syrup (page 185)

Ice, for serving

4 to 6 orange slices

TAMARIND (Tamarindus indica) *is indigenous to tropical Africa. It grows wild in Sudan and is cultivated in Cameroon, Nigeria, and Tanzania. The ripened fruit is used in drinks throughout the continent, as well as in many Caribbean countries. Here, I combine it with orange pekoe tea in a nod to Southern sweet iced tea. Refreshing and delightfully tart, this drink has a faint citrus tang from the juice, smoky caramel notes from the tamarind, and a smooth finish from the vanilla syrup.*

Peel the outer shell of the tamarind pods, then remove the veins from the outside of the fruit. (Compost the shells and veins.) Put the tamarind fruit and the water in a large saucepan and bring to a boil over high heat. Decrease the heat to medium and simmer uncovered, stirring occasionally, for 15 minutes. Remove from the heat, add the tea bags, orange juice, and vanilla syrup, and mix well. Taste and add more syrup if desired. Cover and let steep for 30 minutes. Uncover and let cool to room temperature.

Strain through a fine-mesh sieve into a pitcher, pressing down on the solids to extract as much liquid as possible. (Compost the solids.) Refrigerate until chilled, at least 3 hours. Serve over ice, garnishing each glass with an orange slice.

Menu Suggestions

SPRING

SALAD BUFFET

All-Green Spring Slaw • *page 74*
Cinnamon-Soaked Wheat Berry Salad • *page 102*
Sautéed Snap Peas with Spring Herbs • *page 60*
Verdant Vegetable Couscous with Spicy Mustard
   Greens • *page 113*

SUPPER IN HONOR OF
DR. CARTER G. WOODSON

Gunpowder Lemonade • *page 194*
Teff Biscuits with Maple-Plantain Spread
   • *page 158*
Tofu Curry with Mustard Greens • *page 54*
Spicy Mustard Greens • *page 25*
Vanilla Spice Bourbon Shake • *page 175*
Molasses-Glazed Walnuts • *page 120*

GLOBAL FUSION FEAST

Roselle-Rooibos Drink • *page 197*
Dandelion Salad with Pecan Dressing • *page 81*
Sweet Potato and Lima Bean Tagine • *page 57*
Skillet Cornbread with Pecan Dukkah • *page 131*
Date, Nut, and Cranberry Balls • *page 181*

SUMMER

JUNETEENTH SWEET-AND-SAVORY BRUNCH
(JUNE 19)

Fresh Peach, Banana, and Warm Millet Smoothie
   • *page 155*
Date-Almond Cornbread Muffins • *page 157*
Tropical Fruit Salad with Mango-Lime Dressing
   • *page 179*
Fresh Corn Grits with Swiss Chard and Roasted
   Cherry Tomatoes • *page 160*
Millet-and-Peanut-Stuffed Avocado with Harissa
   Salsa • *page 68*
Jamaican Patties Stuffed with Maque Choux
   • *page 122*
Chipotle-Banana Pepper Sauce • *page 19*

INTIMATE DINNER FOR TWO

Amy Ashwood • *page 186*
Sweet Corn and Ginger Soup • *page 46*
Crispy Teff and Grit Cakes with Eggplant,
   Tomatoes, and Peanuts • *page 104*
Grilled Zucchini with Mixed-Herb Marinade
   • *page 87*
Strawberry-Watermelon Salad with Basil-Cayenne
   Syrup • *page 39*

LIGHT LUNCH

Cucumber-Lemon Water • *page 192*

Mashed Sweet Plantain and Fresh Corn Cakes
  • *page 129*

Hominy and Spinach in Tomato-Garlic Broth
  • *page 44*

AUTUMN

PASSED BITES

Grape-Tarragon Spritzer • *page 193*

Sweet Potato and Pumpkin Soup shooters • *page 47*

Texas Caviar on Grilled Rustic Bread • *page 34*

Crunchy Bean and Okra Fritters with Mango-
  Habanero Hot Sauce • *page 28*

Smashed Potatoes, Peas, and Corn with Chile-Garlic
  Oil • *page 94*

Spiced Persimmon Bundt Cake with Orange Glaze
  • *page 176*

POWER BREAKFAST (IT'S ALL YOU'LL NEED)

Millet and Sweet Potato Porridge • *page 162*

FAMILY FUN FOOD

Berbere-Spiced Black-Eyed Pea Sliders • *page 32*

Ginger-Pickled Green Beans • *page 139*

Za'atar-Roasted Red Potatoes • *page 93*

Ambrosia Ice Pops • *page 168*

WINTER

UMOJA MEAL

Congo Square • *page 189*

Pumpkin-Peanut Fritters • *page 133*

Black Bean and Seitan Stew • *page 50*

Citrus Salad with Arugula • *page 71*

Ginger-Lemongrass Tonic • *page 192*

NEW YEAR'S DINNER

Black Queen • *page 188*

Lemongrass Boiled Peanuts • *page 121*

Stewed Tomatoes and Black-Eyed Peas with
  Cornbread Croutons • *page 53*

Collards and Cabbage with Lots of Garlic • *page 78*

Fig and Pear Pastels • *page 171*

SAINT BOB MARLEY'S BIRTHDAY
(FEBRUARY 6, 1945)

Tamarind Sweet Tea • *page 196*

Creole-Spiced Plantain Chips • *page 126*

Savory Grits with Slow-Cooked Collard Greens
  • *page 108*

Twice-Baked Sweet Potatoes with Winter Salsa
  • *page 98*

Cocoa-Spice Cake with Crystallized Ginger and
  Coconut-Chocolate Ganache • *page 174*

Think Like You Grow

BY MICHAEL W. TWITTY

The great thing about a cookbook like this is that it can challenge us to enjoy the foods we consider part of our culture in new and exciting ways that inform the palate and help us step out of our comfort zone. If you've come that far, I hope I can convince you to go a little further. As Brother Terry has stated, for a long time black people have been the original farm-to-table folks, with some of agriculture's earliest beginnings occurring in Africa. From those roots, our ancestors' determination to maintain their culture and build better lives, even during eras of enslavement and sharecropping, has made us a people rich with the lessons we've learned from the soil and from community with each other. In my experience as a culinary historian of African-American foodways, nothing has shown me our spirit, our determination, and our drive more than our relationship with the land.

In the kitchen gardens of West and Central Africa and from Senegal to Angola, our foremothers raised cassava, yams, rice, millet, sorghum, groundnuts, peanuts, hot peppers, eggplants, tomatoes, okra, leafy greens, melons, cowpeas, sesame seeds, onions, spices, and other foods to create a varied diet. Slave ships carried the seeds of some of those plants to the Americas, where enslaved Africans grew crops familiar to them in what were called truck patches, huck patches, or provision grounds. In mainland North America, our ancestors substituted sweet potatoes for yams, swapped cabbage and collards for tropical greens, added squashes and cucumbers, and made a few other adjustments, while retaining okra, sesame, watermelon, muskmelon, taro, Bambara groundnuts, peanuts, hot peppers, tomatoes, eggplants, and more. Millet and sorghum crossed the ocean, as did balsam apples and pigeon peas. We have one of the longest and most sustained edible gardening heritages in the Americas, and that heritage tells the story of the entire region surrounding the Atlantic.

Whatever the season may be as you're reading this, help carry on that heritage by planning your own Afro-vegan garden. Here's a quick primer to get you started.

PICK YOUR SPACE. For some of us this is a plot in a community garden—and considering how popular they are these days, that may take some planning. You might have a big backyard, or maybe just a small plot or a few pots. Whatever you have, start small and grow into being a master gardener.

KNOW YOUR TOOLS. Basic garden tools include a shovel, hoe, trowel, and rake, along with gloves, pots, stakes, cages, and bricks, blocks, or logs to make raised beds. You'd be surprised how much of this equipment gets recycled, so scavenge for gently used tools before you go shopping.

KNOW YOUR PEOPLE. Gardening can be done as a solitary meditative act, but it works best when we do it in community—with neighbors, family, and friends. Gardening is a great way to hand down food and family traditions to young people, not to mention values such as working hard, delaying gratification, taking responsibility, and being patient. A gardening culture also passes on valuable lessons in history, nutrition, language arts, science, math, geography, and cultural awareness, and does it at a hands-on level.

KNOW YOUR RECIPES. Plant with your meals in mind. Let this cookbook be your guide. You may not have enough space, energy, or time to grow your way through the entire cookbook. However, you do know which vegetables you most appreciate when freshly harvested at peak flavor, and you know what recipes make you sing. Start there. Let the recipes be your guide.

KNOW YOUR AREA AND SEASONS. Zones are usually determined by the number of months you can sustainably grow a food crop. If you live in zones 3 through 6, greenhouses and sunny windowsills are a must. For zones 7 through 12, you can do more planting directly outside and even overwinter some crops, depending on your region and weather. Watch the weather and get to know the seasonal patterns in your area more intimately to ensure growing success. Study your local insects, critters, weeds, and plant diseases, and develop organic strategies for pest control and fertilizing.

SOURCE YOUR SEEDS AND KNOW THEIR STORIES. Okra, black-eyed peas and other cowpeas, watermelon, onions, collards, sweet potatoes, sweet corn, pole beans, peanuts, heirloom tomatoes, hot peppers, pumpkin, ginger, lemongrass, garlic—all are building blocks of a global Afro-vegan kitchen, and all show up in these recipes. The good news is, you can grow all of them in pots, plots, and raised beds. Southern Exposure Seed Exchange, D. Landreth Seed Company, and others focus on heirloom seeds from the Southern tradition and those with uniquely African and African-American histories. These seeds represent an unbroken tradition carried across the Atlantic by our foremothers and forefathers, and their stories can be part of the lessons you learn and pass on to others about our incredible contribution to the American table.

LEARN TO SAVE SEEDS. You can begin to create your own plant lineages by using seeds from the plants you grow. Experiment and see what works. Even if you get only one great tomato and the rest aren't up to snuff, celebrate that. Then save those seeds, and take pictures of the seeds, seedlings, plants, harvested crops, and finished dishes. The best gardeners document what they plant, when they plant it, if they used any tricks to boost the harvest, when they harvested, and how the food tasted. Invest in a journal to keep track of your labors. Most of all, learn to save seeds, storing them in containers that protect against vermin and moisture.

TAKE PRIDE IN WHAT YOU'RE DOING. Being a great gardener is a lesson in patting yourself on the back and loving yourself through good and bad. It's a fantastic way to love your mistakes and learn to laugh at yourself when things don't go right. Enter into your garden space, whatever it may be, with peace and with purpose—and leave with peace and pride, knowing you're walking in the shoes of giants and preparing the way for others to continue this tradition.

Acknowledgments

It takes a village to write a book. . .

Jidan, this book could not have happened without your support. You are such an amazing friend, wife, and mother, and I am blessed to be in partnership with you.

Mila, you are the best thing that ever happened to me! Baba loves you so much!

Mom and Dad, thank you for providing me with such a strong spiritual, ethical, and intellectual foundation. I appreciate you more and more every day.

Jay Jay, no matter how far apart we are, you are always in my heart, thoughts, and prayers.

Mama Wong and Baba Koon, I greatly appreciate all that you do to support Jidan, Mila, and me.

Danfeng, Jando, Chencho, and Alani, it is so great raising our families together.

Bryant Family, Terry Family, and Wong Family, thank you for all your love and support.

Danielle Svetcov, you are a brilliant agent, and I am lucky to have you on my team. Big thanks to Jim Levine, Daniel Greenberg, and everyone at Levine-Greenberg Literary Agency for your support.

Thank you to David Lavin, Sally Itterly, Charles Yao, Tom Gagnon, and everyone at the Lavin Agency for getting me speaking engagements and helping me grow my national platform.

Thank you to the IATP Food and Community Fellows Program (RIP) for providing me with a stellar community of thought leaders and activists and for helping me keep my messaging tight.

I am so honored to be a part of the Ten Speed Family. To Aaron Wehner, for trusting my vision and bringing me into the fold. To Melissa Moore, for being such an amazing editor and kindred spirit. To Toni Tajima, you are the queen of design and can do no wrong in my book. To Kristin Casemore, for sitting down with me in Seattle and being so kind. To Serena Sigona, thank you for putting together such a beautiful package.

Jasmine Star and Sharon Silva, thank you both for your eagle-eye editing.

Heidi Swanson, thank you for being supportive of my work since day one. I appreciate you so much.

Amanda Yee, this book could not have happened without you. In fact, you made it better than it could have ever been without your hard work, intelligent feedback, and expert suggestions for improvements.

Rebecca Stevens, thanks for always being so supportive and giving me feedback on my recipes.

Paige Greene, Morgan Bellinger, Karen Shinto, Jeff Larsen, Dani Fisher, and Rachel Boller, you are a dream team. Thank you for all your hard work creating beautiful images for this book.

Margo Moritz, thank you for the great portrait and lifestyle shots.

Nick James (ICreateForALiving.com), thank you for helping me work through ideas during the early stages of this book. And thank you for adding textures to the portraits of Jessica B. Harris and Romare Bearden, and for crafting the cutting board image of Africa.

John T. Hill and Frank Stewart, thank you for sharing your images of Edna Lewis and Romare Bearden, respectively.

Keba Konte, for allowing us to use your moving photo-montage-on-wood pieces.

Anna Lappe, from BK to the Bay all day.

Jessica B. Harris, I stand on your shoulders and strive to produce work as important as yours.

Michael W. Twitty, your brilliance inspires me to step up my game.

Sophy Wong, thank you for allowing us to use the beautiful fabrics for our photo shoot, and deep gratitude to the many *kitenge* and *kanga* artists, weavers, painters, seamstresses, factory workers, and small family merchants in Tanzania and Kenya who designed, created, and facilitated the sharing of these fabrics with the world.

Polly Greene Webb, your feedback was invaluable.

Luz Calvo, Catriona Esquibel, Matt Halteman, Frederick Douglass Opie, Louisa Shafia, and Supreme Understanding, thank you for your insightful feedback.

Big thanks to all those who tested my recipes at home and offered helpful suggestions for improvements: Beth Bader, Tamara Chukes, Jenny Howard, Donnell Jones-Craven, Gordon Kelley, Josh Paolino, Elise Perlin, Dayna Rozental, Maya Salsedo, Trudy Schafer, Marla Teyolia, and Theresa Warburton.

Kalalea, Kwami Coleman, Dream Hampton, Ferentz Lafargue, David Maduli, and Nicole Taylor, thank you for your inspired music, film, and art selections to help round out this book.

Selected Bibliography

Bower, Ann L., ed. *African American Foodways: Explorations of History and Culture*. Champaign: University of Illinois Press, 2008.

Carney, Judith A. and Richard Nicholas Rosomoff. *In The Shadow of Slavery: Africa's Botanical Legacy in the Atlantic World*. Berkeley: University of California Press, 2011.

Edge, John T. *The New Encyclopedia of Southern Culture, Vol. 7: Foodways*. Chapel Hill: University of North Carolina Press, 2007.

Grant, Rosamund and Josephine Bacon. *The Taste of Africa*. London: Anness Publishing Ltd., 2007.

Harris, Jessica B. *High on the Hog: A Culinary Journey from Africa to America*. New York: Bloomsbury, 2011.

_____. *The Africa CookBook Tastes of A Continent*. New York: Simon & Schuster, 2010.

_____. *The Welcome Table: African American Heritage Cooking*. New York: Simon & Schuster, 1996.

Lewis, Edna. *The Taste of Country Cooking: 30th Anniversary Edition*. New York: Knopf, 2006.

Miller, Adrian. *Soul Food: The Surprising Story of an American Cuisine, One Plate at a Time*. Chapel Hill: The University of North Carolina Press, 2013.

Opie, Frederick Douglass. *Hog and Hominy: Soul Food from Africa to America*. New York: Columbia University Press, 2008.

Samuelsson, Marcus. *The Soul of a New Cuisine: A Discovery of the Foods and Flavors of Africa*. New York: Houghton Mifflin Harcourt, 2006.

Smart-Grosvenor, Vertamae. *Vibration Cooking: or, The Travel Notes of a Geechee Girl*. Athens: University of Georgia Press, 2011.

About Bryant Terry

Bryant Terry is a chef, educator, and author renowned for his activism to create a healthy, just, and sustainable food system. In regard to his work, Bryant's mentor Alice Waters says, "Bryant Terry knows that good food should be an everyday right and not a privilege."

Bryant is the author of the critically acclaimed *Vegan Soul Kitchen: Fresh, Healthy, and Creative African-American Cuisine*, which was named one of the best vegetarian/vegan cookbooks of the last twenty-five years by *Cooking Light* magazine. Bryant also authored *The Inspired Vegan*, and he coauthored *Grub* (with Anna Lappe), which the *New York Times* called "ingenious." Bryant's work has been featured in the *New York Times*, *Food & Wine*, *Gourmet*, *Sunset*, *O, The Oprah Magazine*, *Essence*, *Yoga Journal*, and *Vegetarian Times*, among many other publications. As an exclusive speaker signed with the Lavin Agency, Bryant appears frequently around the country as a keynote speaker at community events and colleges, including Brown, Columbia, NYU, Smith, Stanford, and Yale.

Bryant is the host of *Urban Organic*, a multi episode Web series that he cocreated, and he was a cohost of the public television series *The Endless Feast*. He is a featured expert in the documentary *Soul Food Junkies* and the PBS educational film *Nourish*. Bryant has made dozens of national television and radio appearances, including as a guest on *The Martha Stewart Show*, *Emeril Green*, *All Things Considered*, *Morning Edition*, *The Splendid Table*, and *The Tavis Smiley Show*.

Bryant's education efforts and activism have earned him numerous accolades. In 2012, he was chosen by The U.S. State Department as one of eighty American chefs to be a part of its new American Chef Corps. That same year *TheRoot.com* included him on its list of "100 most influential African Americans," *TheGrio.com* put him on its list of "100 African Americans making history today," and the *San Francisco Bay Guardian* named him "Best Cookbook Cheftivist" in the Bay Area. In 2011 Bryant was included in *Ebony Magazine*'s "Power 100 list," and in 2009, the *New York Times* magazine featured him among a handful of "food fighters." From 2008–2010 Bryant was a fellow of the Food and Society Fellows Program, a national program of the W. K. Kellogg Foundation. Bryant was selected as one of the "Hot 20 Under 40" in *7x7* magazine in 2008, and in 2007, he shared the inaugural Natural Gourmet Institute Award for Excellence in Health-Supportive Education with author and educator Marion Nestle.

In 2002 Bryant founded b-healthy (Build Healthy Eating and Lifestyles to Help Youth), a multiyear initiative in New York City designed to empower youth to be more active in fighting for a more sustainable food system.

Bryant graduated from the chef's training program at the Natural Gourmet Institute for Health and Culinary Arts in New York City. He holds an MA in history from NYU and a BA with honors in English from Xavier University of Louisiana. He lives in Oakland, California, with his wife and daughter. Visit www.bryant-terry.com.

FOR JIDAN AND MILA. YOU ARE THE REASON.

Conversion Charts

VOLUME

U.S.	IMPERIAL	METRIC
1 tablespoon	$^1/_2$ fl oz	15 ml
2 tablespoons	1 fl oz	30 ml
$^1/_4$ cup	2 fl oz	60 ml
$^1/_3$ cup	3 fl oz	90 ml
$^1/_2$ cup	4 fl oz	120 ml
$^2/_3$ cup	5 fl oz ($^1/_4$ pint)	150 ml
$^3/_4$ cup	6 fl oz	180 ml
1 cup	8 fl oz ($^1/_3$ pint)	240 ml
1$^1/_4$ cups	10 fl oz ($^1/_2$ pint)	300 ml
2 cups (1 pint)	16 fl oz ($^2/_3$ pint)	480 ml
2$^1/_2$ cups	20 fl oz (1 pint)	600 ml
1 quart	32 fl oz (1$^2/_3$ pints)	1 l

TEMPERATURE

FAHRENHEIT	CELSIUS/GAS MARK
250°F	120°C/gas mark $^1/_2$
275°F	135°C/gas mark 1
300°F	150°C/gas mark 2
325°F	160°C/gas mark 3
350°F	180 or 175°C/gas mark 4
375°F	190°C/gas mark 5
400°F	200°C/gas mark 6
425°F	220°C/gas mark 7
450°F	230°C/gas mark 8
475°F	245°C/gas mark 9
500°F	260°C

LENGTH

INCH	METRIC
$^1/_4$ inch	6 mm
$^1/_2$ inch	1.25 cm
$^3/_4$ inch	2 cm
1 inch	2.5 cm
6 inches ($^1/_2$ foot)	15 cm
12 inches (1 foot)	30 cm

WEIGHT

U.S./IMPERIAL	METRIC
$^1/_2$ oz	15 g
1 oz	30 g
2 oz	60 g
$^1/_4$ lb	115 g
$^1/_3$ lb	150 g
$^1/_2$ lb	225 g
$^3/_4$ lb	350 g
1 lb	450 g

Index

Copyright © 2014 by Bryant Terry
Photographs © 2014 by Paige Green

All rights reserved.
Published in the United States by Ten Speed Press,
an imprint of the Crown Publishing Group,
a division of Random House LLC,
a Penguin Random House Company, New York.
www.crownpublishing.com
www.tenspeed.com

Ten Speed Press and the Ten Speed Press colophon
are registered trademarks of Random House LLC

All photographs by Paige Green with the exception
  of the following:
Photograph on page viii © by Kristy May
Artwork pages viii, 3, 200 courtesy Nick James
Photographs on pages 2, 58, 114 © by Margo Moritz
Photograph on page 3 © by Frank Stewart
Photo-montage-on-wood pieces on pages 83, 100,
  144–145, 182 © by Keba Konte
Photograph on page 178 © by John T. Hill

Library of Congress Cataloging-in-Publication Data
on file with the publisher

Hardcover ISBN: 978-1-60774-531-0
eBook ISBN: 978-1-60774-532-7

Printed in China

Design by Toni Tajima
Food styling by Karen Shinto
Prop styling by Dani Fisher

10 9 8 7 6 5 4 3 2 1

First Edition